DEDICATION

I **dedicate this book to**

MY WIFE PAT. She told me that our marriage was made in heaven. I really believe that because when Jesus chose me to build a ninety-foot statue of His Mother, He knew I'd need Pat for her help with the statue and with this book. Her support, encouragement, and faith remained throughout both. She called Mary "the Other Woman", but one she never had to be jealous of. My part in this book was easy. I just put the words down on paper; Pat edited and rearranged it.

SISTER MARY JO MCDONALD. When I had finished the face for the statue, Sister Mary Jo came down to Robert's Rocky Mountain yard to see the face. She was so impressed that she asked me if I was writing down what happened each day while I was building it. When I told her no, she said some day people are going to want to know how and why the statue came to be. More importantly, what were the thoughts, feelings, and problems connected to such an undertaking. From that day, I kept a diary. If it hadn't been for Sister Mary Jo's suggestions, I would never have kept notes and would have had nothing to refer back to.

JOE ROBERTS...Our Lady picked each of us for our part in the statue. Joe's part was to be one of the first involved in raising money and to provide a place for the statue to be built. I would like to thank Joe for giving me the opportunity and having the faith in me to build the statue.

A SPECIAL THANKS to the men and women who shared their stories with me: Bob O'Bill, Al Beavis, Joe Roberts, George Nolte, Donna Larson, Bill Barth, Lorraine Childs, Ron Hughes, Dottie Sullivan, Mark Staples, and Marc Comstock.

A SPECIAL DEDICATION to every man and woman who has ever worked for the statue, donated to it, or even said a prayer. Your inspiration, dedication, and spirit were a tremendous force in my deciding to write this book. To the unsung heroes who day by day continue to have faith, perseverance, and a deep love for Our Lady and Her Son, a very special thanks.

ACKNOWLEDGMENTS

PICTURES:

    Joe Vukovich
    Earl Casagranda
    The Montana Standard
    Howard Anderson,
    Tony DiFronzo, Jr. Rainbow Photo
    Joe Sibiga
    Wally Lindquist

A very special thanks to Michael Freze, S.F.O., of Deer Lodge, Montana, for the many hours spent proofreading the original manuscript. His encouragement and suggestions were gratefully appreciated.

Copyright O 1992 by LeRoy Lee. All rights reserved, including the right to reproduce or translate this book, or portion thereof, in any form except for brief quotations in a review.

PROLOGUE

I believe that each of us is put on this earth for a reason. Many search for years and in various ways and places. Others just enjoy life and are open to the whole experience of living. These people are the ones that usually find and recognize their purpose and go on to make the most of it. The people in this book are the ones who have found meaning and have acted upon their instincts in order to achieve their purpose. Some may call them visionaries, others may call them spiritual, and yet others may think them downright out of their minds. Whatever you may think, you have to admit, they are all people who live life to the fullest, believe in themselves, and are not afraid or embarrassed to express that belief. In fact, they put their beliefs on top of the Continental Divide, overlooking the city of Butte, Montana, in the form of a ninety-foot statue resembling the Blessed Virgin Mary. This statue is the symbol of all motherhood, and Mary is the epitome of motherhood. What better reason could there be to place this icon of her for all to see?

The stories related in this book were the personal experiences of the individuals involved. I've tried to be exact in relating the stories as the individuals shared them with me.

What is a miracle? Searching for an answer, I questioned several people. One said, "It is a supernatural happening." Another remarked, "It is an unexplained episode." Still another replied, "When man had done all he could, he trusted the rest to God." The explanation I feel fits this story more than all the rest is: "A miracle is something that can not be explained and changes someone's life drastically." Many things happened to people during the erection of the statue which are unexplainable. Many lives have been changed, some drastically, some just mildly. But they are not the same as when they started, as you can see by the dedication and devotion that is still shown for the Lady and towards each other. Who can explain the turn around for the city of Butte? People's lives were drastically changed for the better. What has happened to each of these people who call these happenings miracles? Their lives have all been changed drastically, mostly in a spiritual sense. So as you read this book, keep in mind what a miracle is to you. Apply your definition to the unexplained. Even though the Catholic Church or any other faith has not put the name miracle on these happenings, it does not mean that a miracle has not taken place. Is not life itself a miracle? Is not belief a miracle?!

Throughout the book, I refer to direct prayers to Mary, and how Mary has answered prayers. This reference in no way refutes the power or worship of God, but instead shows honor to Jesus' Mother as a supreme intercessor. What child has never asked his mother to present his/her request to the father? TO JESUS THROUGH MARY.

TABLE OF CONTENTS

1. Beginnings	1
2. The First Step	5
3. The Mighty Power of the Pen	10
4. Faith Provides the Fuel	14
5. An Eight-Foot Hand	17
6. Work Begins on the Inner Structure	22
7. A Gift for Joe	25
8. "I'll Do It, Joe"	28
9. Our Lady Sends Help	33
10. Taking Shape	37
11. Mary Builds Her Face	39
12. Our Lady Answers A Plea	48
13. Our Lady At Work	52
14. "..If You Knew All That Happened.."	56
15. Sharing of Faith	65
16. Keeping Notes	72
17. What The Lady Wants, The Lady Gets	76
18. The Reluctant Speakers	81
19. Lamb Rock	85
20. A Prayer Group Encounter	90
21. Our Lady Helps Out Again	96
22. Devotion To Mary Pays Dividends	101
23. Christmas 1984	106
24. Our Lady Writes a Song	111
25. "It's Not Broken!"	115
26. The Power of Prayer	119
27. Mary Finds the Keys	124
28. Mary Answers A Mother's Prayer	128
29. Our Lady Provides a Helicopter	134
30. The Big Pour	142
31. The Mountain Is Blest	149
32. Getting Prepared For the Lift	154
33. December 17, 1985 - Day One of the Big Lift	159
34. December 18, 1985 - Too Much Wind	169
35. December 19, 1985 - Near Disaster.	177
36. December 20, 1985 - Tonight's Payday!	189
37. Thumbs Up!	204

CHAPTER ONE

BEGINNINGS

In the big copper strike of 1934, my father, Harry M.Lee, a compressor engineer for the Anaconda Company, was out of work. He and his wife, Alice, went to Missoula, Montana, to live with his brother, Charlie. My dad found work at the sugar factory.

In November, my mother went to Dr. Thornton with stomach problems. Dr. Thornton told her he suspected a tumor and would have to operate immediately. She was admitted to the Thornton Hospital, a privately owned concern on November 9, 1934. Much to everyone's surprise, the tumor turned out to be twins! Because of an earlier pregnancy, in which my older brother had died, my mother was told she would never be able to have children. Now here she was with not one baby, but two! A boy and a girl. According to my parents, we were so tiny, they could put us in a shoe box. We weighed about a pound-and-a-half, and everyone called us the Miracle Babies. We were in the hospital for six months: then we had a nurse for another six months at home. My mother was so afraid of hurting us, she would rather work in the fields with Charlie than try to take full care of us. For years, I remember people telling us how fortunate we were to be alive.

When my sister, Betty Mae, and I were in the first grade, our house blew up due to a natural gas buildup in the pipes. It blew the windows out of houses for over a mile around . My sister and I were sleeping in the same bed when the explosion blew the wall of the house down. The springs and mattress we were sleeping on flew right out from under us, and my sister and I fell on the floor. The frame remained where it was, with us sitting inside it, staring around at the inferno. Finally, taking my sister by the hand, I led her out the opening where the wall had been. A lady noticed us and took us to her house, putting us in bed with her children. My mother and father were in the room which exploded and were badly burned. They refused hospital treatment until they knew we were safe. Several times the firemen entered the flaming building searching for us without any luck. They inquired with the crowd, and finally, the neighbor who had taken us to her home realized they were looking for us. She couldn't understand why everyone was so angry. She hadn't thought about the firemen who had been endangered by entering a burning building several times, nor the pain my parents were experiencing not knowing whether we were alive or not.

We remained in the hospital for a month. My sister and I weren't burnt that badly, but no one knew what to do with us while my parents were being cared for. By the time we left everyone was happy to see us go, as I was not one to sit still for very long. Paper airplanes were one of my favorite pastimes, and I became quite an expert in launching them.

I was always prone to every illness that came along. My sister was accused of giving me all the regular childhood diseases. As a result, I had to miss twice as much school because of the quarantines in those days. School was never an interest to me, maybe because of my falling behind due to illness. Or maybe my parents never stressed it as a valuable asset. Or maybe I was just so interested in life, I didn't understand the necessity of education until later.

My love of hunting and fishing was fostered by my father. Many was the time he took me out of school to go with him. I treasure the times I spent with him hunting and fishing, but I regret the time spent out of school. When I became a senior in high school, I was so far behind in grades, I dropped out of school and found a job.

Although my parents never went to church, they insisted my sister and I go. We were baptized in the Baptist church, but because our parents didn't go, we eventually stopped. I did make God a promise, though, to go with my family when I married. It was a promise I would keep.

I met Patsy Curtin in 1952. We went with each other until 1954, when I entered the U.S. Navy. A year and a half later, I wrote Pat from my ship, the USS Firedrake, and asked her to marry me. Pat was a strong Catholic and the only stipulation she asked of me was that the children we would have be raised Catholic. I had no problem with that. Before going home to be married, I happened to pass a Catholic church in California. On impulse, I went in. After talking to the priest, I decided to enter into the Catholic faith. Pat informed me we would be unable to be married at Mass because I wasn't Catholic. I merely grinned and told her my surprise. This was my gift to her, a unified religion, as well as joining as husband and wife. We were married in St. Mary's Church, which is now the Lady of the Rockies Foundation. We dedicated our marriage to

Mary on our wedding day, never dreaming how important Mary was to become to us.

After being discharged from the Navy in 1958, we returned to Butte, where I became a welder for the Anaconda Company in Anaconda, Montana. We joined St. Ann's Parish where I endeavored to keep my promise to God about going to church with my wife and children. This was easy, because Pat had always gone and would make sure we would continue to do so.

Author LeRoy Lee and wife Pat

In 1962, I transferred to the Berkley Pit garage in Butte. In 1965, I began working for Robert's Rocky Mountain Equipment Co. as a welder. For fifteen years, I worked for Joe Roberts and my life went on in an ordinary fashion, with all the ups and downs of raising a family. We loved snowmobiling, tubing, and visiting with people in the winter. In the summer it was camping, bike riding, and fishing. We lived for the weekends.

My wife and I received two gifts from God when we were in the service --- two precious little girls named Cindy and Kathy. For many years, we felt these were all the children God meant us to have. We decided to help Him a little and adopted a bouncing bundle of joy named Tim. Two years later, we were blest with yet another gift: our son, Rob. Our happiness felt complete. God has been extremely good to us. We have not had any serious illness or problems that He has not been there to help us with. We thank Him every day of our lives.

Pat says she has five children: four who will someday grow up, and me. I still love hunting, fishing, softball, volleyball, bowling, horseshoes, bike riding, etc. I love life!

CHAPTER TWO

THE FIRST STEP

In the summer of 1980, I was in the main shop of Roberts Rocky Mountain Equipment Co when one of the machinists came up to me and said, "Have you heard the latest?"
"What's that?" I inquired.
"They're going to put a statue on the mountain."
"You're kidding!" I exclaimed. "Who told you that?"
"I heard it at the office this morning, and Roberts is involved."
That I could believe! Joe had been involved in many different things. I thought back to the time he had approached me with the idea of the portable building he had seen while in Canada. He described it as one that could be broken down and moved to whatever site it was needed. He assigned me the job of building it whenever I wasn't working on customer's equipment.
When it was completed, Joe planned on using it for building a new home at the Nine Mile. He wanted to start construction inside the portable building because of the weather. A crew installed the frame at the building site of his new home, but before we enclosed it with plastic sheeting, Joe changed his mind about building a new home. We disassembled it and brought it to the shop on Centennial Ave. Still convinced of the idea, Joe decided to install the building in the yard of the shop. Again, we put up the iron frame. This time, we succeeded in partially surrounding it with plastic sheeting. Then a big spring snow storm hit the area. Our spring snows contain a great deal of moisture making it extremely heavy. The weight of the snow became more than the plastic could endure, and the part where the door hadn't yet been installed collapsed. The rest of the building followed, and what was left was a soggy pile of iron and plastic sheeting. I salvaged what I could and the next summer, Joe had me build a green house at his home. The building was reduced from one hundred-feet-by fifty feet to twenty feet-by-ten feet. This time, we bolted fiberglass sheeting to it. If we had

done that in the beginning, we would never have lost the first building. So, like I said, when I heard of the statue, yes, I believed it!

Roberts stopped in the welding shop one day on his way to the paint area.

"Joe," I said, "what's this I hear about you going to build a statue?"

Joe just laughed as he explained it was Bob O'Bill who was planning on building a statue. This was the first time I had ever heard of Bob O'Bill, and as Joe talked, it was evident to me that he had become as enthused about the statue as Bob.

Ann Nettles had called Joe and asked him to speak to Bob O'Bill. Bob had stopped in the office of the Anaconda Company where Ann worked, and in the course of the conversation, Bob told Ann about the promise he had made to put a statue of the Blessed Mother on top of the mountain. Ann told him she knew a friend who also had a devotion to the Blessed Mother and was known for doing the unusual. Ann proceeded to set up the meeting for these two extraordinary men. Because Ann was a special friend whom Joe respected, he agreed to talk to Bob and had become intrigued with the idea. Bob O'Bill knew about Joe Roberts, but he had never met him.

Joe Roberts

Their first meeting was a success, even though Joe expressed the whole idea as crazy to begin with. The more he listened to Bob, the more the idea appealed to him. Joe Roberts attributed this feeling to the expression on Bob's face when he talked about the project. As Joe looked into Bob's eyes, he came to believe that this could be done. Bob impressed Joe with his simple reason for building the statue - He had promised to put a statue on the mountain if his wife survived surgery. Roberts could relate to Bob's feelings, as he is a strong family man and has a deep devotion to the Blessed Mother. Joe believed it could be done, just from listening to Bob O'Bill's sincerity.

When questioned about the size of the statue, Joe stated that Bob had only wanted a small five or six foot one on the East Ridge, but he had convinced Bob to enlarge the measurements. A meeting was planned with other members of the community to discuss the feasibility of the project. Just listening to Joe convinced me that this was something that was going to happen.

A few days later, I saw Joe Roberts again.

It seemed certain there was going to be a statue. At the meeting, Bob Koprivica wanted a cross built and even had pipe to donate for it, but Bob stuck to his decision to build a statue. He said he didn't promise to build a cross, he promised to build a statue of Mary. It had also been decided to involve other people in the community as this was a more extensive project than was first proposed. Bob had picked out a spot on the East Ridge known as Saddle Rock. When I asked in wonderment how they planned on reaching the site, Joe just shrugged and nonchalantly announced they would build a road.

Shaking my head, I went into the tool room to get a drill. I met Ed Monahan and started talking to him.

"Did you hear they are going to put a statue on the East Ridge, Ed?" I said.

Ed said, "You're full of it!"

"No, I mean it," I insisted. "I'm not kidding."

"Where?"

"Come on, I'll show you," I replied as I went to the door. Ed followed me outside to where we could see the mountain and I pointed to Saddle Rock. "See Saddle Rock? That's where they want to put it. I used to hike up there. As a teenager, I hunted the area."

"I still think you're full of it," said Ed.

"I'll bet you ten dollars they're going to put a statue up there!" I countered.

"You're on!" Ed grinned.

A couple of days later, on April 17, 1980, a meeting was held in the conference room of Roberts Rocky Mountain Equipment Co. It was held in order to formulate plans for the erection of a statue of Our Lady of Guadalupe in the Saddle Rock area of the section of the Rocky Mountains east of Butte. Present at the meeting were Bob O'Bill, Joe Roberts, Art Korn, Joe McCarthy, Sid Hughes, Sheila Penaluna, Bob Koprivica, Ernie Cesarani, Dan Ramirez, Bill Dorr, Al Beavis, and Ann Nettles. Ann Nettles was appointed secretary. Bob O'Bill opened the meeting by distributing reports of letters from the U.S. Department of

Agriculture which showed areas of mining claims. Bob had checked with the courthouse and found that particular claim was owned by the Ossellos of Butte. Bob submitted a picture of the Saddle Rock area along with a letter to the Department of State Lands of the State of Montana requesting a notarized Small Mines Exclusion statement and a copy of the affidavit of their request. Joe Roberts, in the meantime, was working with some architects in Spokane on details of the structure of the statue.

Joe advised the group of the donated equipment, which would be necessary to build the road to the site and also the clearance of the working area. He expressed how lucky they were to have Sheila Penaluna working with the group. Sheila had taken pictures of the site by air and had drawn the statue near the planned location.

During this meeting, it had also been decided the statue's measurements would be sixty-feet tall, twenty-six feet wide, and twelve-feet thick. It would be fabricated with steel, wrapped in wire mesh, and coated with plastic. It would be pearlized white in color in order to show up on the skyline. Sheila suggested the features of the robe be exaggerated so that as the sun changes, shadows would accentuate the details. She would design and supervise construction of the statue.

Bob O'Bill

The eight-thousand foot altitude could present a problem because of the snow depth in the winter. Not only would the workers have to contend with the snow, but also temperatures of thirty to forty below, along with the wind factor. All this did not dampen the committee's enthusiasm for the statue. In fact, the nice part of it being that high would make the area inaccessible during the winter and lessen the chances of vandalism. The only people who might find their way there would be snowmobilers, and they felt these people, along with hunters, would not be interested in destroying a monument of this nature.

The possibility that ARCO could be approached to help in the project was also brought up, but the general consensus of all present was that the endeavor was to be for the people of Butte. They all believed there would be sufficient enthusiasm and donations from the people themselves. No one had any idea how much money would be involved, but all felt it would be a costly venture.

The first step would be the road. Joe Roberts volunteered to build the road with the machinery he had if in the yard. Bob O'Bill would talk to Frank Gardner from the Anaconda Company and hoped to be assured of some equipment from them at no cost. The group would make the stipulation to pay for the fuel and supplies if ARCO agreed to this. It was decided that fuel could be furnished from donations that would come in. Bob Koprivica and Joe Roberts each donated the sum of one thousand dollars for fuel and other expenses. Labor would be furnished on a voluntary basis from whomever believed in the project.

A lot had come out of this first meeting. It looked like the statue had gotten the "go-ahead" signal.

CHAPTER THREE

THE MIGHTY POWER OF THE PEN

For the next year, things were fairly quiet concerning the statue. Bob had put together the site preparation crew consisting of Al Beavis, Bill Dorr, Mike Cerise, Pat Regan, and himself. On May 1, 1981, Bob and some of the others ventured to the mountain and endeavored to reach the proposed site. Snow and mud on the north side of the mountain prevented them from attaining their goal. Even though they were expecting it, they were still disappointed. They had hoped to break through the barrier of snow and mud to formulate their plans for the summer. Leaving the site, they made plans to try again later in the month.

In the meantime, Joe Roberts traveled to Spokane to work with a design engineer. Marvin Orgill, a good friend of his, had been contacted and was willing to help in the design, composition, and building of the statue. Marvin came up with the dimensions of ninety-feet tall, thirty-six feet wide, and sixteen feet thick. On hearing this, I could not help but be amazed!

"Joe, do you know how tall that is?" I exclaimed.

"Yes, as big as the tallest building we have here in town," Roberts said proudly. Nothing would daunt this man and his dream, not even a ninety-foot statue! Once Joe got involved with anything, he was like a dog with a bone. He would not give up. The Lady had picked the right promoter for this project.

By the time the snow had finally left the mountain, Bob had gone to the Anaconda Company and had received equipment valued around two hundred fifty thousand dollars, all of which had been obtained as a donation. Dave Barker, an employee of Roberts, picked up the equipment and brought it to Roberts for servicing. All this time, I had heard of Bob O'Bill, and as yet had not met him. I finally got to see the man I had heard so much about. What impressed me most was how lively and enthusiastic Bob was. Here was a man with a dream and a purpose. Everyone who would meet this man would become as enthusiastic and committed to the project as he was. The feeling was contagious. This was a man who would not ask any more of you than he was willing to do himself. Dedication and determination flowed out of Bob O'Bill like a river and engulfed anyone who expressed a desire to help. Once you had been touched by these qualities, you became as engrossed in the project as Bob was.

Dave Barker hauled the equipment to the mountain, and Joe Roberts donated the use of the shop pickup to Bob O'Bill for transportation to and from the mountain. Bob would get off work, and he and the others would begin their long evening on the mountain preparing the road for the site. Many were the times they came back hours after dark, tired and hungry. The faith of these men amazed me. Here they were building a road and the statue was not even started. They had no way of knowing if the statue would ever become a reality, yet here they were night-after-night, week-after-week, struggling to blast through rock, and grading for a road they believed would be used to build a statue on the mountain. These men gave of their evenings, their weekends, and even their vacation time in order to make a dream come true. True dedication? True determination? You bet! These men were the inspiration for all who came later! These were the real statue builders, the ones who conceived the statue a reality. How could we give any less when it was our turn to do our part?

Another unsung hero was George James, a parts man for Roberts. He put in his time during the day, and at night became a watchman for the yard. This meant that whenever the men on the mountain were through, they would bring the truck back to the yard to be serviced and fueled for the next day. George, no matter what time of the night it happened to be, would have to open the gates and see that everything was locked up again. I'm sure there were many nights he would have loved to have gone to bed instead of staying up to open the gates for them. He never complained though. At times I got the impression that George James didn't really believe the statue would ever be there, but then, so did a lot of other people. Dreamers were what Bob and his crew were called. At this stage, I wasn't sure about the statue, either. It really seemed like a far out idea.

On August 29, 1981, an article appeared in <u>The Montana Standard</u>, a local newspaper, stating that a big statue was to tower ninety feet over the Continental Divide. I read it, but never gave it much thought. Later, I realized that article just about destroyed the whole project. The article stated that Bob O'Bill had approached Joe Roberts some time ago after Joyce O'Bill, Bob's wife, had survived a serious illness. It went on to say how a road had been cut across the Continental Divide, east of Butte. Blasting had begun into solid rock for the base of a ninety-foot high tribute to the Virgin Mary. Roberts had been quoted as envisioning a tramway up the mountain. The statue was to cost one million dollars, and the tramway two million dollars. The next morning I could hear Roberts shouting all the way to the welding shop.

"What's wrong with Joe?" I asked one of the machinists.

"He's upset with the piece in the paper," one of them remarked. Knowing Joe would eventually be down to the shop, I just bided my time. Sure enough, Joe stomped in a little later.

"Did you see that piece in the paper?" Roberts shouted. Without waiting for a reply, he continued, "I could take that reporter and hang him!"

"Why?" I asked.

Roberts' eyes were flashing as he answered, "When I was asked how we were going to finance the statue, I said it would be with donated help and equipment. Then the reporter asked me to put a price on it if it were to be paid by money. I told him about one million dollars for the statue, and approximately two million dollars for the tramway. Then he has the audacity to conveniently forget I said it would be all donated time, money, and equipment. Now everyone thinks it is going to cost that much. No one knows it will all be donations. We're going to hear about this one!"

Boy, was he right! At this particular time, Butte and Anaconda were in a depression. The smelter, which was one of the largest industries in the area, had just closed. Thousands of people had been affected, either directly by losing their jobs, or indirectly, especially by businesses supported by the workers. Everything pointed to Anaconda, (and possibly Butte) becoming ghost towns if the mines closed, and here it is announced that a project costing three million dollars is to be undertaken for the sole purpose of putting a statue on the mountain. Upsetting? That was an understatement! Our local newspaper has a section called "Our Readers Speak", and boy do they speak!

Esme Labreche wrote: "I cannot imagine how people of conscience can plan to place a ninety-foot statue on the Continental Divide at an estimated cost of three million dollars when there are people in need. Federal Government cuts are to be made in Social Security, and elimination of monetary assistance in paying power bills."

Christine Tilman said, "..better uses for time and money. Some people vision the statue on the East Ridge as a shrine to religion. When I see this statue, I see a tourist trap. I shudder at the thought of the destruction of one of God's natural wonders. The money could go to the schools, outdoor ice rinks..."

Ray Calkins wrote "..Who would pay for future upkeep? It would become a monument of rust, just a lightning rod for the mountain.."

Pauline Wood called Joe on the telephone requesting him to stop work on the project to allow a short time for community reaction to die down.

Sandy Clayton wanted to build the statue somewhere else. Yet, for all the adverse reactions, there were also some very supportive ones.

Kathy Gonzales wrote, " the statue will add more beauty.."

"Looking forward to the statue..," wrote Pat Patterson.

Don Serich remarked, "Other towns would welcome the statue."

What was really upsetting though, was the effect it was having on the O'Bills. People would call their home at all hours of the day or night to make objectionable remarks. Joyce got to the point where she would no longer answer the telephone. It was extremely disturbing to her. The Roberts' family was experiencing the same venom from compassionless people. This whole controversy existed because of a false report in the newspaper. Oh, the mighty power of the pen!

CHAPTER FOUR

FAITH PROVIDES THE FUEL

Many things happened that are unexplainable. Two of them didn't become clear to me until later when I had a chance to ponder them. The first one occurred when Jack Warner, the shop foreman, came to the welding shop and told me to prepare the welding truck to disassemble some one hundred-ton trucks that belonged to the Anaconda Company. They were being shipped to Wyoming and needed to be disassembled so they could be put onto hauling trucks. Dave Barker would take the crane, Jim Dunn the transport, and I the welding truck. Upon arrival at the site, we were all amazed to see so many trucks. During the preparations of taking them apart, we started to drain the oil from one of them. The oil was like new! On further investigation, we also noticed the antifreeze was as good as when first put into them. On an impulse, I went over to the fuel tanks, and much to my surprise, they were full! When we returned to the shop that night, I went to see Joe Roberts, but he had already left. The next morning, I made a point to catch him before we headed out again.

"Joe, you won't believe this," I said, "but every one of those trucks' fuel tanks are full of diesel. Bob O'Bill could sure use it on the mountain for the equipment."

When Joe heard there were about five hundred gallons or more in each tank, he directed me to obtain fifty gallon barrels to drain the fuel into. On further report of the oil and antifreeze being new also, we were directed to salvage the fuel first, then the oil and antifreeze.

I couldn't believe it. We salvaged twelve barrels every night. We'd load them on the transport and take them to the shop. When Bob O'Bill came down and saw all the fuel, he thought he had died and gone to heaven. Here he had more fuel than he knew what to do with and all these months he'd barely had enough. He hadn't known from day to day whether he would have enough for the next night or not. Because he'd had faith throughout this whole time, the Lady provided him with all the fuel he needed.

The second unexplainable episode happened in July, 1981. Joe Roberts came into the welding shop one morning and told me Al Beavis had talked the Anaconda Company into selling a load of pipe for three hundred dollars. He was excited about the amount of pipe they had received for that price. Roberts had sent Dave to get it before they changed their minds. When Dave returned with the pipe, I took a look just out of curiosity. I, too, was surprised at the amount of pipe for the price, but never gave it another thought after that. The pipe would serve as another reminder of the Lady taking care of the project as she saw fit.

In the meantime, Joe and Bob had found a sculptor in Butte who consented to build the statue. He would begin by making a ninety-inch model to work from. When completed, he would use it to build the statue on the mountain. At the time, I thought they wouldn't have much time for building it, as time was limited by the weather and the short summer seasons we always had. Winter always came early and left late. The high altitude would also have an effect on the workers.

"Joe, what have they decided to build the statue out of?" I inquired one day.

"Well, we talked about fiberglass, but Bob had a dream one night and someone set it on fire, so that took care of that idea. Cement was a consideration, also, but we finally decided on iron," Roberts explained.

As the months passed, every once in a while I would ask Joe how the statue was coming. Joe Roberts and Bob O'Bill had gone up to look at the model, but weren't impressed with the face. The sculptor insisted he could fix it by smoothing it out with lead. Bob volunteered to get some for him.

A few weeks went by, and Roberts kept me informed of the progress. The face improved, but the statue looked as though it were wearing a suit of armor.

When the statue was completed, the sculptor brought it down to Roberts' yard and put it in the used parts warehouse. Since everyone was looking at it, I went too. As I stood there looking at this statue, I was impressed: not because of its beauty, but with the work that had gone into it. As a welder, I could appreciate the time and skill that it had taken. I couldn't, even in my wildest dreams, imagine how it would look ninety-feet tall. I remember thinking, "What a job that's going to be!" I could see ninety inches, because a person can stand and work around it, but ninety feet? I remember thinking, "I'm glad he's doing it. I wouldn't know where to start."

"Hey, LeRoy, what do you think of it?" I turned around to see Roberts standing there.

"Boy, he put a lot of work into it, didn't he?" I replied.

"Sheila Penaluna looked at it and wasn't very impressed," Joe said. "She thinks it's out of proportion."

As I looked at it, I could see she was right. If the statue could put its arms down, they would hit the floor.

"She's right, but what impresses me is the work that has gone into it," I exclaimed.

CHAPTER FIVE

AN EIGHT FOOT HAND

One morning Joe Roberts walked in and invited me to accompany him to the old Ryan Mine in Walkerville. The Anaconda Company had given it to The Lady and Joe wanted to see if we could use the iron for her.

When we arrived there, I couldn't believe it. The Anaconda Company had started a building and had never finished it.

"Joe, do you have any idea what all that iron is worth?" I asked.

"Yes, I just wanted to see if we could get it down," he answered.

"You get Dave Barker up here with a crane, and we'll get it down," I exclaimed.

"That's what I wanted to hear!" Joe happily announced.

A few days went by before Joe brought Bob O'Conner's brother, Tom, an ironworker who was temporarily out of work, to help dismantle the building. The next day, Dave, Jim Dunn, O'Connor, and I went to Walkerville to begin dismantling the building. When we climbed to the top of the structure, Jim and I couldn't believe how high we were. You could hear our knees knocking and shaking. O'Connor walked around the beams like a cat, while Dunn and I crawled on our hands and knees hanging on for dear life.

"I wonder if I'm going to live through this?" I remember remarking to Jim Dunn. I kept seeing myself falling.

"Don't feel lonesome!" Jim shakily answered.

As the days went by, Jim and I became more brave and even started walking the beams like O'Connor. It was something a person had to get used to, I guess, --- as long as I didn't look down.

As we disassembled the iron, we hauled it to Roberts' yard. When it was all in a pile, we couldn't believe how much iron we had. The Lady had been generous again.

Joe came into the shop and invited me on another excursion. This time to the used parts warehouse where the statue was.

"LeRoy," he said, turning to me, "do you think you could build a ninety-foot statue from this?"

"Probably, if I had the prints and grid," I replied.

"There are none. The sculptor just made the statue. He didn't go by any plans," Joe remarked.

I stared at Joe.

"You're kidding! I wouldn't even know where to start," I exclaimed. "Could you build a statue looking at me?"

"Well, no," Joe admitted.

"That's what you're asking me to do, Joe," I replied. " I've never sculpted anything in my life."

"So you don't think it can be done?" Joe challenged me. I gave the matter some thought. I never could pass up a challenge, and this certainly was in that category.

"Let me see, Joe," I answered hesitantly. "I'll try to build a hand and see how it goes."

"Why a hand?" Joe asked.

"When I was in art class in high school, I always had trouble drawing hands. If I can make a decent hand, there may be a chance. Can you see how much fun I'll have making one that big?" I grinned.

"Give it a try. That's all you can do," Joe said, grinning back.

For days after that, I became obsessed with my hand. I'm sure people thought I had lost my mind altogether. I walked around looking at my hand, moving it to see how many different ways I could turn it. I had never really thought about my hand before, but now it seemed to consume me with the different functions it possessed. I needed to make a grid for the correct proportion of the fingers to the hand. I decided to use six-inch pipe for the fingers. A problem arose because of the weight of the pipe. The exhaust pipe we had in the shop was four-inch and lightweight, but where would I ever find six-inch exhaust pipe? I recalled we had some one-hundred ton truck salvage in the scrap yard, and I hastened over to it. Sure enough, there was enough to build one finger.

Now my attention focused on my finger. Do you have any idea how many lines are in your finger? There must be hundreds! Talking to myself as I went, I decided to start with the fingernail. I cut the pipe on the sides and bent it down. Surprisingly, it looked like a fingernail! Making more cuts I bent the pipe so it would look like a bent finger. When Roberts came in and saw it, he laughed.

"Look at the size of that! How big is it?" he asked.

"Five-feet long and six-inches wide. What I'm going to need now is more pipe and plate," I replied.

"What's the plate for?" Joe wondered.

"For the bottom and back of the hand," I said.
"How heavy?" Roberts wanted to know.
"Fourteen gauge," I answered.
"Well, get what you need," he said.
"By the way, Joe, what about the statue? What are you going to do for iron for that? That's going to take tons of plate," I said.
"That's right. Why don't you start looking into it? Get some prices on fourteen gauge from different places while you are at it," Joe replied.

A month before Mother's Day in 1982, Roberts was planning to place the ninety-inch model on display in the Copper King Inn. He had me build a stand to enable people to view it better. On impulse, he decided to take the finger so people could envision how big the statue would be. We loaded the finger in the back of the truck. People stared and pointed to the appendage as we brought it out. It was pretty funny, now that I think of it.

After the display, Joe shared some of the remarks made by the people who had viewed the statue. Many thought it was crude, but donations still poured in which went to the road building fund. A lot of the comments were about the finger. No one could get over the size of it. It just blew their minds to think of a statue that large!

When the pipe arrived, I initiated building the fingers. Upon their completion, I took the plate, cut the fingers on the back end, enabling them to slip over the plate. Slowly the structure started to look like a hand. After the thumb was built and the bottom plate in, I returned to the salvage yard and picked out a piece of twenty-four inch pipe to make the wrist. I bent it into an oblong shape and welded it on. Everyone coming into the welding shop was amazed how huge the hand looked. They had thought one finger was large, but when they saw the hand, everyone started to realize just how enormous this statue was really going to be! Everyone said the same thing: "If the hand is this big, I can't wait to see what the statue will look like!"

When Joe Roberts came in, he got all excited. "Get it in the paint shop and get it painted," he exclaimed. "LeRoy, is there any way we can smooth the welds?"

"I don't think we should grind on them any more, but if we put auto body filler over them, when they are sanded and painted, you'll never see the welds," I said.

"Good idea!" Joe said. "Get Joe Sibiga and Ron Lyons to do it."

Sibiga started it, but other jobs demanded his attention, so Ron Lyons finished the body work and painted the hand. When the hand was dry, I couldn't believe how nice it looked. I thought to myself how proud I was to have built it. I had been working and building things out of iron all these years, but this was something thousands of people would see and would know I built. At this stage of my life, I wasn't able to acknowledge any of the help the Lady had given me. I was still full of self-pride. It was a feeling I had never felt before, and as the machinists and others from the office came down to look and pat me on the back, it really didn't mean much. The men I wanted to please were Joe Roberts and Bob O'Bill. Joe saw the hand first. I could see he was pleased. He didn't even have to say anything --- just seeing his face was enough.

"LeRoy," Roberts said, "put it in front of the office for Christmas. This will be our Christmas gift to the people of Butte." So I put it on a pallet, got the hyster, and with Ron Lyons' help, we took it to the front office. I had to weld an angle to the post holding the front porch. We then tied the hand to the angle. Joe came out and asked, "How much do you think it weighs, LeRoy?"

"Oh, about two or three hundred pounds, I'd say."

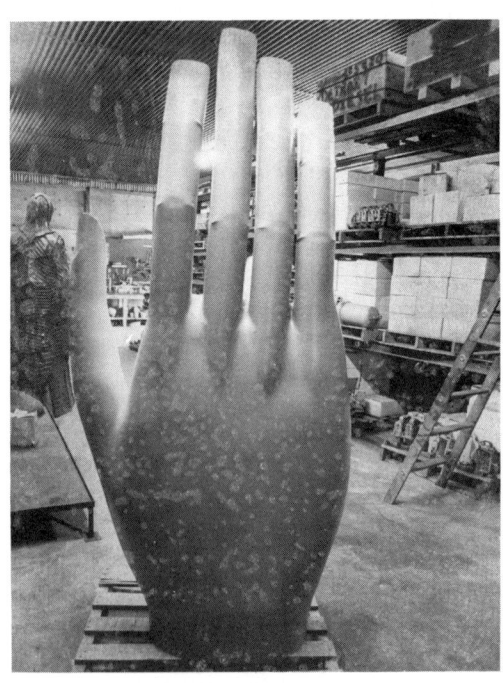

The right hand, and in the background, the first nine-foot model

"You know what we need?" Joe said. "A steel box to take in donations. We'll put it outside the gates so when people come down and the gates are locked, they can still donate if they want," Joe explained. I went down, built the box, and welded it on the post so no one could take it.

When Bob O'Bill came down to get the truck, he came in the welding shop. He had a big smile on his face and said. "Good job, LeRoy!"

"It did turn out good, didn't it?" I grinned sheepishly, delighted that I had pleased Bob.

It was unbelievable how many people stopped down to see the hand and how the donations mounted. The people of Butte at long last could visualize the project they had been donating to and were able to realize that it would actually become a reality, not just a dream.

CHAPTER SIX

WORK BEGINS ON THE INNER STRUCTURE

Months passed. Joe Roberts discussed with Al Beavis, Mike Cerise, and Bob O'Bill the difficulties they were having constructing the road to the statue. Winter set in and work stopped for the duration of the season.
 In the spring of 1982, Joe asked me to assess the pipe that had been brought down from the Anaconda Company. We wandered around taking mental notes of the dimensions of the pipe as we looked.
 "How about it, LeRoy? Do you think you could build the superstructure for the statue from the pipe we have here?" Roberts inquired, hoping for the right answer.
 "Me? What happened to your friend Marvin Orgill, the architect in Spokane? I thought he was supposed to donate the plans for it," I answered with great surprise.
 "You know how that goes," Joe replied. "It's been almost a year now. I'm not going to wait any longer."
 "Hmm... Well, I'll see what I can do, Joe. Do you have any ideas how you might want it constructed ?" I said.
 "If we build the structures in six pieces, then they could be separated," Roberts said as he mulled over the idea in his head.
 "Yeah, that might work. It would sure be easier to work with. How high do you think each piece should be?" I questioned him.
 "How about ten or twelve feet each?" Joe answered.
 "I'll measure them and see if that will work," I said.
 "Yeah," He said. "If we can separate them into six sections, it would be a lot easier to move them to the site. Then we can put them together on the mountain. Yeah, that's what we'll do. See what you can come up with, LeRoy, and let me know." Joe said as he ambled back to the office.
 As I stood there, looking at the piles of pipe, I thought, "Where in the world do I start?" After much deliberation, I finally decided to see what kinds of pipe I had and how much there were of each kind. Looking at

that varied from thirteen inches in diameter to twenty-two inches in diameter and was one-fourth inch thick. I figured I could get six sections from what I had if I made them twelve feet high. It would come out at seventy-two feet. This would approximate the length up to the shoulders in comparison to the ninety-inch statue.

I hurried into the yard, moved a bunch of equipment, and drew a line seventy-two feet in length on the asphalt. I extended the line twelve feet on each side from the bottom, and eight feet on the top, then drew a line from the top to the bottom. Joe Roberts happened to wander into the yard just then. I beckoned to him and he changed direction toward me.

"What do you think about this? Should the statue be twenty-two feet wide, or twenty-four feet?" I asked after I had explained what the lines were for.

"Let's go twenty-four feet," Roberts said after some deliberation.

"O.K.," I said. "Now that I know the angles, I can go ahead and cut them. There's some used sheets of plates over there that we can use for the plates on the bottom of the pipes."

"Do you think they will be heavy enough?" Joe asked.

"If we bolt them together it would double the thickness, and then we could weld them together when the statue was done. Besides, when you don't have any money, you use what you have," I replied. Joe agreed.

When I wasn't working on customer equipment, I'd be working on the pipes for the inside structure. As I finished, I put them out along the side of the paint shop.

Months passed. Work went on as usual with Bob O'Bill on the mountain. The inner structure proceeded slowly at the shop. Joe Roberts came down one day and told me Bob needed some welding on the "Cat," a piece of equipment, on the mountain. I was delighted, because now I would get to see for myself how much work had been done on the road. Bob was happy to see me, not only to fix the equipment, but to also ask about the statue's structure. After getting an update, Bob expressed his desire to help on the statue, but would be unable to until winter set in and closed the road for the season.

"Boy, I'm really impressed with the road, Bob. That's a lot of work! How come you built the road down the mountain and not across it?" I inquired.

"When we got through the cut, we thought about going across the mountain, but the rocks were so big, the "Cat" couldn't push through, so we took the easy way. Afterward, Lavelle Powder Co. donated all the powder we needed. If we had had it in the beginning, we probably would have gone straight across," Bob replied. "But, it's there now, so that's where it will be." On the way down the mountain, I was glad I had the chance to see what they had done on the road and to feel the excitement that emanated from Bob and the crew that worked on the mountain.

Winter came on, and the snows closed down the road project again. True to his word, Bob and his crew showed up every night at Roberts' shop to help with the structure. At first they just drilled the plates, then I showed Bob how to use the large wire welder so they started putting the plates on the pipes. After a large pile of pipes had accumulated, Bob brought Bob O'Connor down and we started to bolt the pipe structure together in a long line. Then Al Beavis brought his son, Randy to survey them to make sure they were straight. Once that was done, we were able to start the cross bars. Again, I went to the pile of pipe. All the large pipe was used, except for the six inch. The trouble was that the one-half inch walls made them heavy. Since that was all we had, we used them.

CHAPTER SEVEN

A GIFT FOR JOE

Things weren't going very smoothly with the sculptor and Roberts. Every time I saw Joe, he seemed to be angry with him for one reason or another. Finally, I asked him the reason why he was so upset. The sculptor had found a buyer in Washington. Since the Foundation had paid him nineteen hundred dollars for the material, they felt it was not his to sell.

Even Bob O'Bill was unhappy with the sculptor. In the course of a conversation, he had expressed how important the sculptor would be once the statue was completed. Bob, being an unassuming individual, insisted that this statue isn't to glorify anyone but the Mother of God. This attitude disturbed Bob a great deal.

The sculptor had become quite angry with me also when I wanted to sandblast his statue and paint it white. He felt he made it and he should be the one to decide what to do with it. He was going to put clear lacquer on it so it wouldn't rust, but that was all.

Several days passed before I saw Roberts again. He felt relieved that the sculptor had been taken care of. It had been decided to just let him have the statue ending the transaction and preserving the attitude with which the project was started. The statue wasn't being built for monetary gain, but for the honor of Mary for a promise that was fulfilled.

A few days later, I bumped into Bob O'Bill.

"I hear Joe gave back the model," I said.

"Yeah, after I saw his statue, I went home and said a prayer to the Lady. I told her I didn't think this was how she was supposed to look. I asked her to find someone else," Bob said. I marveled at his firm belief.

One day, when I was in Roberts' office, he showed me a picture of Our Lady of Guadalupe given to him by Bob O'Bill.

"Did Bob tell you the story behind Our Lady of Guadalupe?" Joe queried.

"No." I answered, quite intrigued with the question. I was always interested in whatever Bob O'Bill was involved in.

Joe thought for a minute, then started speaking, "When Bob's wife, Joyce, was ill, Bob was worried sick. The doctors informed him she needed an operation, with only a fifty-percent chance of survival. Needing someone to talk to, Bob sought out his friend, Dan Ramirez, and poured out the whole story. Dan asked Bob if he had ever prayed to Our Lady of Guadalupe. Dan, then went on to tell Bob that she is the Mother of all and answers all our prayers. Bob, being desperate, said he would try anything. The next day at the hospital, as Joyce was being operated on, Bob remembered what Dan had told him about Our Lady of Guadalupe. Right then and there, Bob made his promise. If Joyce were to recover, he would build a small statue in Mary's honor. That's how the whole project came about, LeRoy. So you see, we have to preserve the spirit of Bob's promise."

"That's a beautiful story, Joe. It just goes to show you what the power of prayer will do," I commented. I could see then, why the picture of Our Lady of Guadalupe meant so much to Joe. Bob O'Bill had given it to him in remembrance of his promise.

I kept thinking about the picture as days passed. For some reason, I couldn't get that picture out of my mind. Thoughts kept creeping in about the statue's properties. Maybe it needn't be a three-dimensional statue. Maybe it could be made flat as it would be seen from the town from only one angle. All sorts of ideas kept popping in at the most inopportune times. It was weird. I finally found a picture of Our Lady of Guadalupe and drew it on a piece of steel. The figure was two-feet high after I cut it out. I placed a face in it, then hands. Intrigued with the idea, I cut two side pieces for the veil, then welded them to the piece of iron. Still not satisfied, I leaded the face and hands, making them look white, and braised the rest of it. Feeling quite pleased, I showed it to the guys and told them we could give it to Joe at our Christmas party coming up.

All the years I had worked for Joe, we had always had a Christmas party. But this year because business was slow, Joe had decided not to have one. When the employees heard this, they were at first disappointed, but then they decided to put on the party themselves. Everyone agreed that giving the sculpture to Joe would be a wonderful idea.

At the party when the sculpture was presented to Joe, everyone could tell he was quite touched. Joe, being a man of deep feelings, was at a loss for words --- one of the few times in his life. Afterwards, Joe thanked me personally. He expressed how touched he was by the whole evening, but felt bad because his employees had to put on the party this year. Joe was a proud man, but it made all the employees feel good to think they could give something back to this man.

The next Monday, Roberts sauntered into the welding shop.

"You know, Joe," I wondered aloud, "why not put a statue like the one we gave you last Saturday night on the mountain?"

"What about the back of it?" he said, interestedly.

"We'd have to put a pole or something in back to stabilize the structure so it wouldn't blow down. Maybe some kind of a tripod shape." I answered.

"No, I don't think that would work," Joe said. "We hope someday people will be able to go there to see it. It will just have to be a three-dimensional statue, somehow."

One day as I was working, the face of the statue entered my thoughts. I wondered how hard it would be to make a face from iron. Finding a piece of five-inch pipe, I tried bending it to a shape of a face. I positioned the eyes and mouth, then placed a veil around the head. When completed, I stood back and laughed. Joe happened to arrive at the shop just then, and I expected him to laugh also. Instead he just looked.

"How long did it take you to make that?" he inquired.

"About four to six hours," I answered, surprised at his reaction.

"Hmm, that's pretty good," he said, and walked out. He must have liked it, because he kept bringing different people in to show it to them. I set it on one of the cabinets and one of the machinists started calling it the "goo goo" lady. One day when I arrived, she had a hard hat on her; another day, she had a mustache, and finally she had on a pair of safety glasses. She looked like a welder. Everyone got a laugh from it. Every time Bob O'Bill came in he'd ask me if he could have it. I don't know why he wanted it.

CHAPTER EIGHT

"I'LL DO IT, JOE"

I was working in the welding shop when Bob O'Bill came in. In his hands, he held two ceramic statues of Mary. One was ten-inches tall, the other fourteen inches.

"Hey, Bob, what are you planning on doing with them?" I asked, pointing to the statues.

"They were given to me. I thought you might like to see them," Bob answered.

I thought to myself, "I've seen statues before. What's the big deal?" Bob set them on the work bench and started to leave.

"Hey, Bob! You forgot your statues!" I yelled as he went out the door.

" I'll pick them up next time I'm in," Bob said, looking over his shoulder, continuing towards his vehicle.

"But they may get broke in here," I protested.

"I'm not worried," he laughed, and then he was gone.

Going over to where Bob had placed the statues, I picked them up, looked them over, and decided to put them on a higher shelf, all the time muttering to myself, "Sure was dumb of Bob leaving them here in the welding shop with me. Be just my luck to break them."

As the days passed, I kept walking by and looking at the ten-inch statue. For some reason, that statue kept drawing my attention to it every time I went by. The larger one didn't even get a second glance, but the ten-inch one seemed to pop out at me even when my mind was on something else. One day I paused and really took a good look at it. I picked it up, examined it carefully, and thought to myself, "If the ninety-inch model looked like this one, we would really have something." The more I peered at the statue, the more I felt that this was how the Lady of the Rockies should look. Then the thought crossed my mind: Is this why Bob brought these statues down here? Did he have the same thing in mind?

One afternoon Joe Roberts walked in.

"What are you doing? Anything?" he said. All the years I worked for Joe, he always said the same thing when he came in the welding shop. "What are you doing? Anything?" Some things never change.

"You're just the guy I want to see!" I exclaimed.

"What do you need, LeRoy?" Joe inquired.

" Joe, look at this statue Bob brought down last week." I reached for the statue and handed it to him. "This should be Our Lady of the Rockies," I insisted. Joe took the statue, turned it slowly in his hands, and gently caressed it.

Ten inch model from which statue was built

"We thought about a statue with its hands out, but we thought the wind would be too strong, putting too much pressure on it," he remarked as he kept looking at the statue.

"Look, Joe, the way the statue is built, the wind would blow up and across her bust, and if we put screen in the veil, the wind will pass right through. If we paint it white, from a distance you never would know the screen was there," I said, pushing the idea. Joe kept turning the statue around and around in his hands. As he turned it, you could see the wheels turning in his head along with the statue.

"The ninety-inch model had her hands in prayer. If the people stood on the ground looking up at her, they wouldn't be able to see her face. Also, how would you light her so the shadows won't cover her face?" I continued with my questions.

"This is one reason the sculptor and I weren't getting along," Joe replied. "I wanted to drill holes in the hands for a light so the face would be lit up, but he said no." Joe still held the small statue in his hands, turning it absent-mindedly. "I like this statue. I wonder who we can get to design and sculpture it if we decided to use this?" Joe was thinking out loud. Out of the blue and out of my big mouth, came the words...

"I'll do it, Joe." Where those words came from, I didn't know at the time. But as the years passed, I knew Our Lady gave them to me.

"Do you think you can?" Joe said incredulously. He was as stunned as I, but yet I felt he had confidence in me even at that time.

"I built the hand and it turned out well," I replied. "I'll take this little statue home, put it into a grid, and we'll go from there."

Joe didn't say anything. He just stared at me. I wasn't sure what he was really thinking, but he was smiling, so I figured he liked the idea.

"What about the hand? Will you have to build a new one, or can you use the same one?" Joe asked.

"No, I'll just turn it down. It should work either way," I replied after some deliberation.

After some thought, Roberts said, "Go ahead! What do we have to lose?"

When Joe left, I thought to myself, "What in the world did I do? I'm no sculptor. I didn't even finish high school." When I had first heard about the statue, I remembered thinking "How could anyone build a statue that big from iron?" And then I go and tell Joe that I'll do it! All of a sudden, I wanted to run after Joe and tell him I was just kidding; but on the other hand, I thought, "Wouldn't it be something to build a statue that big?" The more I thought about it, the more enthusiastic I became. My thoughts kept running rampant. Joe must have faith in me to let me try something as big as this. I wonder what Bob O'Bill and the rest of the men will think? Will they try and talk Joe out of it, or because I built the hand will they have faith in me too? Things were running through my mind, one after another - fear, excitement, doubt. I kept asking myself,

"What have I done?" I was having a hard time getting my mind back on the job I was supposed to be doing.

When quitting time came, I couldn't wait to get home to share the news with my wife, Pat. I thought, "Will she believe me?" When I walked in the house, I had the little statue in my hand.

"What are you doing with that?" Pat asked.

"I'm glad you asked," I said smugly. "I'm going to build a ninety-foot statue from it."

"Sure, you are, LeRoy," she said.

"No, really, Pat," I tried to explain.

"You're not a sculptor," she replied.

"Well, I've got to start somewhere. I built a hand, didn't I?" I said testily.

"That's a long way from a ninety-foot statue," Pat insisted.

"You're right, but it's worth a try. What have I got to lose? I can always tell Joe I can't do it, and he can find someone else. But I'm going to try," I said with confidence.

"If you want to do something bad enough, then you'll do it," Pat remarked. "By the way, where will you start?"

"The first thing I have to do is establish a grid, so I can keep it in proportion," I said.

I could barely eat dinner, I was so eager to get started. I sat the little statue down, and stared at it. The more I stared, the more I lost faith in what I was doing. Pat suggested that I use graph paper for the grid.

Since we didn't have any in the house, I had to wait until the next day. That night in bed, I must have built twenty statues in my dreams. But when I woke up, I was still back at square one.

The next day, I saw Roberts. "How's the statue coming, LeRoy?" he asked.

"I'm going to put it into a grid first. I should be able to start on it tonight when I get the graph paper," I replied.

"Go for it!" he laughed.

As the day went by, I became more eager to start. That evening, taking a measuring tape, I measured across the statue's face to the outside of the hair on both sides. I then realized I was going to have to use fractions. Oh, great! In school, fractions were my worst nightmare. I always did them in my head at work. I never could do them on paper. So, as I started to put them down, I would double-check with Pat, who is a teacher.

"How did you ever get that?" she would ask. "I've never seen anyone do it that way before. Let me show you how to do them." What a mistake! It really is true, you can't teach an old dog new tricks. No matter what Pat did, it didn't make sense to me. I always went back to the way I was used to doing them. We would sit there and argue all evening. Finally, we realized we both came up with the same answers. After a good laugh, we decided the best way to figure it out would be to do the fractions the way each of us were comfortable with, then compare our answers. If we both arrived with the same answer, we would be doubly sure we were right.

I was amazed that one-half inch would come to four feet, six inches on the ninety-foot statue. Now I was ready to put the Lady on graph paper. With my ruler, I'd measure the statue, then transfer the measurements to graph paper. Night after night, as soon as dinner was over, I'd work on the grid. At long last, I had the front, back, and both sides of the statue completely gridded.

I took the grid to work to show Joe.

"When will you start the real thing?" Joe inquired.

"I figure I can start as soon as the structure is completed," I replied. I put the grid on the cabinet door in the welding shop, telling myself, "This was the easy part. If I never do anything else, at least I have done this much."

When Bob O'Bill came in, I showed the grid work to him. He just smiled. I really think Bob knew something I didn't. Why he brought those statues down in the first place was still a mystery to me. He never did tell me, but afterwards I recalled he was not very comfortable about the ninety-inch statue from the beginning. He went home and prayed to Mary, telling her that she had to find someone else to build the statue. The ninety-inch model wasn't what he had in mind. I had to laugh. Could it have been me? What a paradox! I know if I was going to have something built, I sure would get someone who had experience and knew what he was doing. I thought to myself, "Here is a sculptor who makes beautiful small sculptures, has experience, yet he had trouble with a ninety-inch statue. I never made anything before, and here I am attempting a ninety-foot statue." I really have to be out of my mind! Oh, well, I have to get the inside structure done first. I can worry about that later.

CHAPTER NINE

OUR LADY SENDS HELP

In May of 1983, a young man about 30-years-old entered the welding shop of Roberts Rocky Mountain Equipment. He looked around until he spotted me working on a gusset for one of the pieces of the structure of the statue.

"Hello," he shouted above the noise of the welder. Looking around, I noticed a medium built man about five feet, ten inches tall, with a scruffy beard and a big grin on his face scrutinizing me. I never dreamt at the time how much help this man would be or what good friends we were to become. "Are you LeRoy Lee?" he continued.

"You're looking at him," I replied.

"They told me at the office you were the one to talk to," he said.

"What can I do for you," I asked.

"I'm Ron Hughes," he said, sticking his hand out. "I understand you need some help on the statue."

"I sure do! Are you a welder?" I questioned.

"I'm trying to be," he grinned.

I thought to myself, "I wonder what he means by that?"

Ron, who lived in Anaconda, Montana, had been going to Vo-Tech in Butte to learn how to weld. He had heard about the statue at school and had come to volunteer his services for a few hours every day after school. Reluctantly, he admitted he could only run flat welds, but was eager to try overhead and vertical welds.

"Don't worry. We'll have a lot of flat welding, and you can do anything you feel comfortable with," I answered, just glad to have the help. Later on, I found out he had worked in Anaconda for a beer company for ten years, but was now unemployed. It had been a great job, and he could work on the trucks as a machinist, a carpenter, or almost anything they asked him to do. He had run into a little bad luck when the owner, a boss he'd really liked, decided to retire. The son replaced the father in the business, and things were not as pleasant around there from then on. Ron had to decide whether to remain under those circumstances, or quit and find work elsewhere. Ron chose to find work elsewhere, even though work was scarce in that area.

After much soul searching, Ron decided to become a welder. So far, he had two quarters in at the Butte Vocational School. When he had heard about the statue, he decided he could learn the trade much faster by volunteering his services. Besides, it intrigued him to be able to work on something that big and learn how to fabricate in large dimensions.

After we became acquainted, I gave him a tour, and showed him the pipe structure that we had put together.

"We have hundreds of plates to make and drill, then we'll weld them on the cross bars. Still want to help?" I laughed.

"You bet! Thanks, LeRoy," he said. "I'll see you after class tomorrow night."

As the weeks passed, Ron would come every afternoon for two hours. One morning as I went to open the welding shop, there was Ron!

"What are you doing here?" I asked

"I don't have the money for school anymore; besides, I'm learning more here than I was at school. So if you don't mind, I'd like to help all day if I could," Ron answered.

"Great!" I exclaimed.

As the weeks passed, I could see much more getting done on the statue frame. I couldn't work on it all the time because when a customer came in, I'd have to stop and take care of the customer. Both Joe Roberts and Bob O'Bill were delighted that Ron donated so much time. Then one morning Ron made a sad announcement. He would no longer be able to donate his time. His money had run out, and he was unable to drive over every day.

I pleaded with Ron to wait at the shop while I hurried over to the office to talk with Roberts.

After explaining Ron's dilemma to Joe, he offered to take twenty-five dollars out of the donation fund for gas for Ron's vehicle.

"Hey, Ron," I shouted, "come over here. If the Lady gave you twenty-five dollars a week for gas, would you be able to come?"

"Yes," he answered, grinning.

A few more months went by, and once again Ron came to me with a problem.

"LeRoy, I'm sorry. As much as I love coming here, I just can't afford it any longer. I'm falling way behind in my bills, and I just have to find some kind of a job. I really hate to leave now that I can see the statue making progress, but a guy has to eat, too," Ron stated morosely.

So once again, I started off to find Joe. He was in his office when I asked to see him.

"You know, Joe, Ron is becoming a fine welder," I started out. "You keep telling me about all these volunteers who will show up to help weld on the structure, but where are they? Bob O'Bill can't help because he's busy working on the mountain, using all the men who have volunteered. Ron is doing a great job, but he has to quit. He needs to look for a job to pay his bills and eat on. Is there anything you can do about keeping Ron here?"

Roberts thought for a minute, then said, "Well, the donations have been coming in pretty good since the hand went out in front at Christmas. We could give Ron one hundred dollars a week if he'll stay on," Joe offered.

When I told Ron, he was delighted. So was I. It was nice working with someone like Ron. When Bob O'Bill came down, I told him what Joe had done. I was wondering what he would say because the money was coming out of the donations, and that would be less money for the mountain and equipment. I explained the situation to Bob, and how I was unable to work full-time on the statue. It was imperative to work on customer's equipment . Roberts had to keep the place operative, as business was at an all-time low everywhere. If the statue was going to be completed, we would need help. Bob agreed. I was glad, not only for the help, but also to help Ron.

Ever since the Company cut back its operations in 1980, then shutting the smelter in Anaconda that fall, work had been slow, and all the businesses in Butte had been affected. We had received work from the Anaconda Company, and then from the Arco Company, who bought them out. The parts department was a going concern. Rumor was strong of the Butte operation being eliminated. If that were to happen, we would all be unemployed, with no opportunities for other jobs as Butte was a one-industry town. Roberts felt the strain of the impending closures deeply, as most of his employees had been with him for years and were like family to him. If there were any way to keep Roberts open, Joe would do it. I believed him because I had seen hard times before when his partner Les Sheridan was killed in a plane crash. Every one thought we were going to be looking for another job, but Joe wouldn't let it happen. He put the company back on its feet.

Then in the fall of 1983, the worst happened. Arco suspended all its mining operations in Butte. The town was devastated. Jobs were ending everywhere, but Joe managed to keep us all working. I don't know how he did it. I'm sure he was hurting as badly as the rest of the businesses. Bob O'Bill, Bill Barth, Mike Cerise, and Bob O'Connor became unemployed. Because of their skills, they were able to find other employment.

With the Company shut down, many hard times were in the futures of the men and women of Butte and Anaconda. These people had experienced many hardships in the past, but this seemed to be the worst disaster that could happen. Many contemplated leaving even though their hearts were in Butte. Sad times for families seemed imminent. Something needed to happen to enrich the hearts and souls of those who decided to remain and find some kind of livelihood. Everyone's faith needed restoring.

CHAPTER TEN

TAKING SHAPE

Joe Roberts came into the shop with a piece of good news.

"LeRoy," he said, "I found a place we can get a good buy on fourteen-gauge steel which we need for the statue. The only problems are we have to buy five thousand dollars' worth, and its located out of state. I'd have to send Dave Barker down with the transport to get it."

"That's a good deal, Joe," I replied. "I'm surprised you can get four-by-ten sheets for that price. That's a lot of iron, but at that price, you'd be crazy not to. Look at the money you'd save in the long run!"

"Yeah, but there's a little matter of finances," Joe thoughtfully remarked. "I'd have to get a loan from the bank and hope we get enough donations to pay for it. I'd really be taking a risk."

As Joe slowly walked away, I thought to myself, "I'm glad it's Joe worrying where the money is coming from, not me."

Ron Hughes kept building cross bars for the structure, and I would help when I wasn't working on a customer's equipment. After several months, the inside structure was beginning to take shape, and Joe Roberts was becoming impatient to show the people of Butte what was being accomplished. He wanted to put the structure together in the yard. I felt it would be too high, but part of it might be feasible if we had some kind of base to situate it on. Joe's excitement bubbled over and he said he would get Dave Barker to clear a spot for the base.

Sure enough, the next day, Dave moved all the equipment across from the welding shop, cleaned the area, and leveled it. Then Dave brought his transit and shot the holes so the base would be square.

About that time, a young man named Randy Wixsten was hired as a shop boy for Roberts. I hesitate calling him a boy because his six-foot, three-inch frame towered over all of us. Randy was a good looking young man of nineteen years and proved to be invaluable with his many talents. Joe Roberts told me to put him to work, and I did --- digging holes for the base.

Later, I saw Bob O'Bill and quickly ran over to where he was.

"Hey, Bob," I yelled at him, "is there any more pipe at the Anaconda Company yard?"

"Why?" questioned Bob.

"Roberts wants to stand the structure in the yard. He feels it will make people stop to see what's going on. He expects it to help donations come in better," I answered.

"Gee, LeRoy, they gave us all they had," Bob replied. He thought a moment and then said, "Wait! I have a piece Frank Gardiner gave me for stoves across the street; maybe you can use that."

When I saw it, I couldn't believe my eyes. It was twenty-four inches diameter and ten-feet long! Just enough to get four legs to make the four-foot skirting that the next twelve-foot section would sit on.

After Randy dug the holes, we poured cement around the pipe in order to support the structure. When the cement dried, we started to assemble the structure pieces. Dave worked the crane; Randy, Ron, and I bolted them together. It was incredible how big the four-foot section and the twelve-foot section looked when assembled. But that was as far as we ever went. The structure was never all together until it was on the mountain.

Bottom of inner structure

CHAPTER ELEVEN

MARY BUILDS HER FACE

It was the first part of October, 1983, when Joe Roberts came into the welding shop to see how things were going.

As always, he said, "What are you doing? Anything?" After explaining what I was working on, he asked, "When do you plan on building the statue?"

"Oh, maybe next week, when things get caught up around here. I still have a few more things to do before I can start," I replied, not really having thought much about it.

"What are you going to start with?" Joe wondered.

"Probably the face," I glibly stated.

"Well, whatever you do, make her pretty because if you don't, the statue will never succeed. People won't donate to it if they don't like how she looks," Roberts said.

"I'll do my best, Joe," I said. When Joe left, I thought to myself, "Well, you opened your big mouth. Now what are you going to do?" Apprehension came over me. As the day went by, I kept thinking about the face, and apprehension turned to anticipation. I couldn't wait to get started. By Wednesday, having caught up with my work, I entered the paint shop where Dave had put all the four-foot-by-ten-foot, fourteen-gauge sheets of iron. I brought one sheet into the welding shop, then removed from the shelf the small statue Bob had brought down. I scrutinized the face, then I examined some more. I studied and studied, but the only thing I could think of was, "Where in the world do I start?" The forehead looked about the easiest, so I referred to my grid. My God! The forehead was eight-feet wide, not counting the hair! So I began. -And as the day passed, and the next, and the next, I realized I was hopelessly bogged down. I thought, "Thank God, it's Friday!" I was disgusted as I went home. Walking dejectedly into the house, I quietly went over to my reclining chair. Pat noticed something askew.

"What's wrong? You look like you lost your best friend!" she exclaimed.

"I'm no sculptor!" I exploded. "Pat, I took on something I don't know anything about."

"You built the hand," she pointed out.

"Yes, but that was only eight-feet tall. This face is fifteen-feet tall and ten feet wide! I've worked on it for three days, and I still don't have any idea what I'm doing. Monday, I'm going to tell Roberts to find somebody else," I declared sadly. Just the thought of doing that made me nauseous. All this time, I had given everyone the impression I could build the statue. It was hard to admit defeat. Jack Warner's words kept going through my mind. He didn't believe a statue would be built. In his opinion, we were just wasting the money people were donating to it.

The next day, Saturday, I went hunting. I had a hard time concentrating on elk, as I still felt terrible about letting everyone down. As I walked along, I arrived at a final decision. There was no way I could build the statue. The first thing Monday morning, I would tell Joe I did not have the skill to do it.

That afternoon, after returning home, Pat asked me whether I wanted to go to the 4:30 Mass that evening, or wait and go on Sunday. At this time of my life, going to church was a duty. I could take it or leave it. It was the only thing my wife asked of me and the kids, that we would take time out of our life for one hour a week and give it to God. I was like Hipshot Percussion in the newspaper funnies. I'd rather give my prayers to God in the mountains He made, not a church that men made. I told Pat we'd go to the 4:30 Mass that evening because I wanted to go hunting Sunday.

As I sat in St. Ann's Church, I may as well have been on top of a mountain someplace. I wasn't getting anything from the service. I noticed the statue of Mary and Baby Jesus on the wall. Being a convert, I had never said a prayer to Mary. When I did pray, it was always to God. I felt you should go to the One in power, not take a side street to someone less. But for some reason, I felt compelled to say something to this statue of Mary.

"Mary, if you want me to build a statue of you, you have to help me," I implored. Then I dismissed it from my mind. The night was spent like any other evening --- dinner, putter around in the garage, watch some TV, take a bath, and go to bed. But sleep alluded me. I tossed and turned and thrashed about. All I could think about was how I would tell Joe Roberts and Bob O'Bill they had to find someone else. It was terribly unsettling. But then, my mind started to think of the face. I could see myself cleaning the welding shop floor, drawing a one-foot grid and drawing the face on it. I took flat strap and bent it into half an egg, using the grid to keep it in perspective. When that was done, I welded the fourteen-gauge plates together and drew the same grid on it. Then, I proceeded to draw the face, side view, forehead, nose, mouth, and chin. I cut them out and inserted them onto the half-egg frame. I became quite excited. I wanted to wake Pat up, but I thought otherwise. I decided to wait until morning instead and establish the plans more firmly in my mind. Finally, morning came, and I was still excited.

"Pat," I said, as I saw her coming to life, "I think I know how to build the face of the statue! It came to me last night as I lay thinking."

"Did you have a dream?" Pat asked.

"No, I knew I was awake. I couldn't get to sleep, and I tossed and turned all night. It was like watching a movie. I can't wait to get to work to start. I know how to build it!" I exclaimed happily.

Monday, when I arrived at the shop, Ron Hughes was already there, waiting for me. He knew how disgusted I had been when I left Friday night, so he was surprised at my exuberant manner when he saw me. He had been convinced I was going to tell Roberts to find someone else when I had left Friday. Now he didn't know what to think after seeing me so happy.

"Get the broom going. We're going to clean the floor," I barked. He looked at me quizzically, because it wasn't that dirty.

"What are we doing?" he asked, puzzled by my actions.

"We're going to build a face!" I stated.

"By cleaning the floor?" he replied.

"Ron, I know how to build the face," I insisted. He just looked at me. I could tell what he was thinking. Friday I didn't know what to do. What had happened over the weekend? Before he could say anything, I said, "It just came to me like I was watching a movie. Everything was laid out and just came pouring into me. Let's get going!" He didn't say a word; he just got a broom and started to clean the floor. When the sweeping was done, I told Ron we had to calibrate the floor into one-foot squares, eighteen-feet long and ten feet wide. Then I sketched the face in the squares. I took and bent one-and-one-half by one-eighth flat iron around her face and made the half egg shell.

"What is THAT?" Joe asked, coming into the shop and seeing the egg shape on the floor.

"The face," I exclaimed.

"It doesn't look like anything to me," Joe said, giving me a look like I was crazy.

"It will," I replied laughingly.

The next day, I was still enthusiastic about the project. We lay three, four-by-eight sheets on the floor and tacked them together. I designed the side view of her face on the sheets, then cut it out. When we put the side view on the egg shell, it started to look like we knew what we were doing. I couldn't wait until Roberts came down again. It wasn't long before his curiousity brought him back. When he saw it, he became elated.

"Now I see what you're doing. My God! look how big it is! It fills up the whole welding shop," he blurted out.

As the days went by, I couldn't remember ever having as much enjoyment as I had when I was working on the face.

In ceramics, Pat had created a face of a woman. It was larger than the statue I had to work with. At night, I would study the face with my fingers and my measuring tape. I asked Pat if I could take her ceramic head to work. She agreed, but cautioned me not to break it. (She knows me too well!) Around the shop I started measuring the back of the heads of all the machinists. They would see me coming with the tape measure and hurry and put their hats on. Here comes crazy LeRoy! That didn't stop me, though. Actually, I think they got a kick out of the whole thing.

The fraction conversion chart I had made came in handy. All that arguing and figuring paid off. If a piece would measure one-fourth of an inch, I'd look it up on the chart and find out I needed to cut a piece of iron two feet, nine and three-fourths inches. I filled the whole face with iron and it looked like half an egg. Ron would follow me and wire weld the pieces of plate I had put in.

Hunting season was in full season by now. Every year I would take a week's vacation to go hunting. This year I wondered if I could possibly leave the face long enough. By working long hours and only leaving long enough to get some sleep, I felt far enough ahead of myself to sneak in a week of hunting. Ron would be able to weld on the pieces until I returned. After a week of hunting and wondering about the face, I returned to find Ron had welded all he had to do, but was unable to continue until I returned. In the meantime, he worked in the main shop and built a wood stove for the paint shop. He was pleased to see me because he was anxious to see how the face was going to look.

The first thing I started on was the nose. Wow! It looked just like Porky Pig's nose. We all had a good laugh over that one. Instead of being round, it was flat. Joe was a little upset.

"What are you going to do about it?" he demanded.

"Cut it apart and do it again," I laughed. The next day I cut the nose apart and redid it. This time it looked like a nose. From there I proceeded to the forehead, while Ron continued welding on the nose. The forehead went smoothly, and the next maneuver was the eyes. Everyone felt that I would have trouble with the eyes, but they also went effortlessly. The mouth was next. I had no idea how many ways a mouth protruded until I started it. I must have situated nine pieces of iron in the mouth. I examined lips, everybody's lips I could. What a variety there is in the world! Some big, some little, some skinny, some fat. I must have seen them all, and not a one was alike.

About this time, Ron came to me with a downcast face.

"LeRoy, I'm in deep trouble. I'm going to lose my house. I'm deeply in debt, and I owe everyone in town. The hundred dollars I'm receiving just isn't enough. That Chevy truck goes through gas like you can't believe," Ron confessed.

"Ron, I don't know how you could live on one hundred dollars. Let me talk to Roberts and see if I can get the amount raised," I said. I left for the office immediately. Joe was in his office when I asked to see him.

"Joe, Ron needs more money to live on or he's going to have to leave. I hate to see this happen because he's an awfully good worker and we really need him," I stated.

"I feel badly about Ron, but we just don't have the money to pay him more," Joe replied. I went back to the welding shop and told Ron the bad news. He became quite morose.

"Ron, I know if Joe had the money, he would give you more," I tried to pacify him.

"Well, I can't afford to come any more. This will be the last you see of me!" he said as he trekked out of the shop.

When I went to work the next morning, I was disappointed to find Ron not there. I felt awful and thought how lucky I was to still be working. Customer work just wasn't coming in. Even the machinists were on part-time. It seemed like ever since the Anaconda Company shut down, the whole town hasn't had much work. It had really hurt Roberts because of the parts he sold to the Anaconda Company. It is particularly sad at Christmas time for people to be laid off. But we all say when the statue of the Lady goes on the mountain, Butte will turn around.

I started the chin of the statue by putting the straps in. I was just putting the plates on, when Roberts came into the shop.

"How's it coming?" he asked. "Do you think you'll have the face done for Christmas, LeRoy?"

"I don't know, Joe," I said. "It's going a lot slower without Ron to help. Now when I get the pieces tacked in place, I have to go back and weld them, too. Ron used to do that." I wanted to tell Joe how much I missed Ron, but I knew there wasn't anything Joe could do. I know the day he came down and found Ron had left, he felt bad.

About a week went by and Joe bounced into the welding shop. He had a big smile and said, "Can you get in touch with Ron? Donations have been coming in more abundantly because of Christmas, and we can afford to pay Ron more now." I was so elated, I could have kissed Joe. Instead, I volunteered to drive to Anaconda that evening and tell Ron myself. "Tell him we can pay him two hundred dollars," Joe continued.

After supper, I drove to Anaconda. Ron was surprised to see me. After I gave him the good news, he was overjoyed. As we talked Ron told me how depressed he had been. He had missed not working on the statue. He wanted to come back, but his pride and lack of money prevented him. His brother kept encouraging him by telling him things would get better. With a huge grin on his face, he said that his brother was right. They did get better. After talking some more, it was finally time to leave. Ron informed me he had no money for gas, and he didn't know how he would get there in the morning. I gladly gave him some money for gas .

The next morning, Ron was surprised to see the face almost completed.

"Boy, that looks good!" he exclaimed.

"It's coming," I said proudly. Ron finished the welding while I put her veil on. Then came time for the hair. I thought about using cable for it, but it wouldn't have looked like the little statue. I thought of cutting plates and overlapping them. I decided to try overlapping; sure enough, it looked great. Ron voiced his approval along with Joe Roberts. When the hair was half way down her face on both sides, I had to stop. I couldn't go any further until the shoulders were built.

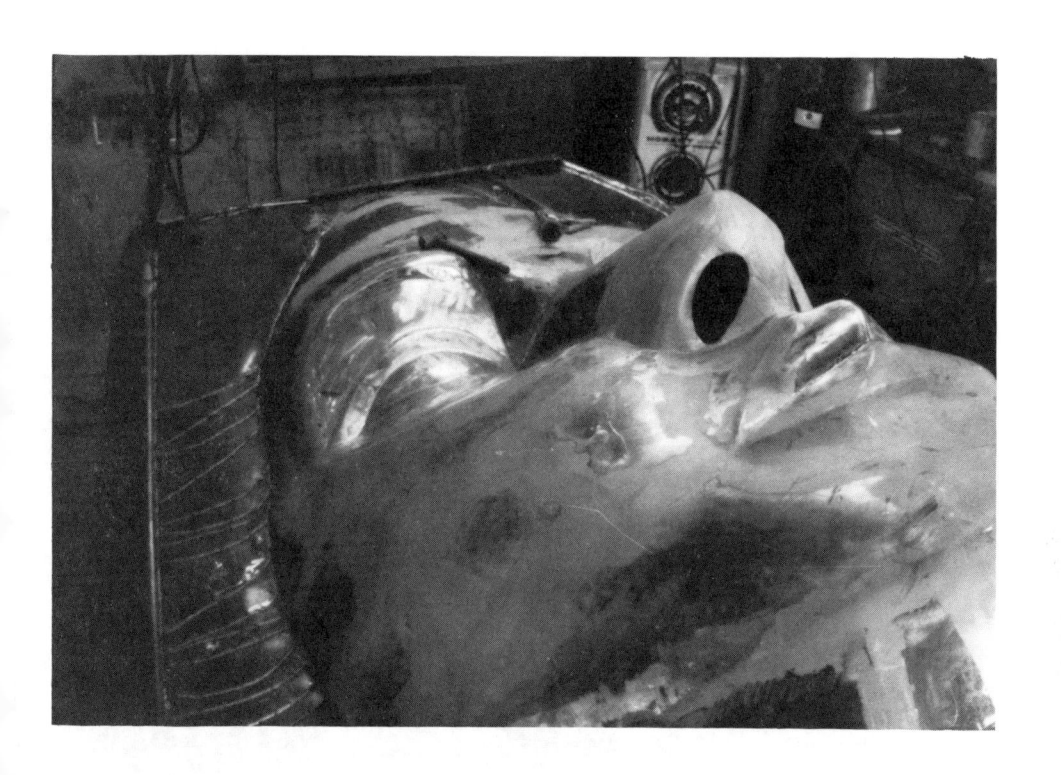

Face and hair

"We want the face smooth, like the hand you made, LeRoy," Joe suggested.

"Randy was telling me about a new body filler they use on cars called aluminum fill. It's not supposed to rust," I said.

"Order some," Joe said. When it came, Joe Sibiga and Randy Wixten put the aluminum fill over the welds and sanded it down to prepare it for painting. Ron Lyons and Randy painted the face. When it was dry, we were all astounded. She was beautiful! My thoughts went back to the time I was in church and said that prayer to Mary. I wondered if the prayer had anything to do with what I had just accomplished. Or in my foolishness, did I plan to take full credit for myself? I just didn't know. But I do know that we all stood there in awe at the magnificent face we were beholding. Roberts insisted we take the face out to the front of the office so everyone could see her. All the office came out to look. When Bob O'Bill saw it, he smiled from ear-to-ear. The people of Butte came in a steady stream from that night on, and donations reached an all-time high. What a beautiful Christmas gift we gave them. At last they could see where the donations were going and how pretty she was going to be. As Joe and I were having our pictures taken with the face, Joe looked at me and said, "You do as you're told. I said make her beautiful or people won't donate. Well, we're not the only ones that think she's beautiful because the donations are pouring in."

I thought back to the beginning. My family would tell people that I was building the statue, and people would call them liars. It was getting so bad they wouldn't say anything to anyone any more. Everyone was under the impression that the original sculptor was still building the statue.

Randy Wixten, LeRoy Lee, Joe Sibiga, and Ron Hughes

After Christmas, Joe decided not to return the face to the welding shop because donations were still coming in regularly. In order to keep Ron working all winter, I felt it was necessary to keep on building pieces separately. We had pieces for the back of the head, the veil, and the neck all over the shop, even extending into the paint shop. Since we still didn't have access to the face, our next move was to start the shoulders. Ron and I cleared out the welding shop because we needed thirty feet of space for the shoulders. If a big job came in, we would have to work outside, which did not appeal to either of us during the winter months.

We worked industriously on the shoulders for a time. It began to look as if we were building another building inside of the shop.

"Are you building a ship inside a bottle where you can't get it out?" Joe inquired, concerned about the hugeness of the structure.

"No," I replied, "I measured the door before I started and it will just fit when we take it out."

"How do you plan on getting it out?" Joe exclaimed, puzzled at the whole idea.

"Easy," I insisted, chuckling all the while. "We'll put pipe under it and roll it out. Nothing to it." Joe just shook his head and left the welding shop. Ron and I laughed. To us, the solution seemed very simple. I guess to someone else, the problem looked as large as the shoulders. And they were large! If you weren't aware of what they were, you would think we had lost our minds. The shoulders resembled a large Quonset hut sitting inside of the shop.

CHAPTER TWELVE

OUR LADY ANSWERS A PLEA

Even after having been shown how to build the face, I was still a "doubting Thomas" about the talent involved in the construction. Was it a gift from Mary, or did I really possess the ability to construct the face on my own? This was a question that haunted me from time to time. Being human, and a novice at believing in miracles, I occasionally boasted of the great job I had done. Then, something happened that jolted me into the realization that miracles do happen, and it was not an accident or a hidden talent that I possessed which caused the face to be built so beautifully.

George Nolte, a very close friend of mine, had drawn a special elk permit to hunt in Yellowstone Park in January of 1983. As he was preparing the camping trailer for the trip, he slipped on the ice. Severe back pains caused him to lose his breath as he struggled to his feet. Eventually he was able to make it inside the house where he took some aspirin to ease the pain. After an hour or so, the pain subsided and he was able to stand and walk gingerly. George had a history of back problems, so he called his chiropractor, Dr. Philip Blom. Dr. Blom, decided to take x-rays before proceeding with the treatment. When viewing the film, the doctor was puzzled. Thinking the film had been overexposed, he took another set of x-rays. They came out the same way, just a faint image of the backbone with a vertebrate broken . After a consultation, Dr. Blom referred George to Dr. Speckert in Missoula, Montana. George was very apprehensive, as he knew Dr. Speckert was a cancer specialist.

During the initial visit to Dr. Speckert, several tests were taken and George anxiously waited for the results. A week or so dragged on with images of the worst possibilities invading his mind at all times of the day and night. Sleep became impossible and fear lay heavily on his heart. Then the dreaded news came. His worst nightmare became a terrible reality. Dr. Speckert informed George he had atypical cells in his bone marrow. It was a myeloma, a form of bone cancer, which in five years would in all probability result in death. A cold chill engulfed him as he tried to comprehend what this all meant to him. Then he started lashing out and questioning.

"Why me? WHY ME?" He raged on in his mind at the unfairness of it. Here he was, in the prime of his life, only forty-six years old, and so many things he still wanted to accomplish. With great resentment, George fought against all efforts people made to help him feel better. How did they know how he felt? They weren't the ones who were dying! After a period of this self-pity, George realized what this was doing to his family. He decided to make the time he had left count for something and to enjoy what he was able. He started to act like his old self, again making jokes, and giving people a bad time. George's sense of humor is a rare treasure, and everyone was delighted once again to experience his love of a good practical joke. But all was not as it was before. Very quietly, George started making plans. He started to give individuals in his family the material things he wanted them to have. His hunting guns, his equipment for fishing, anything that meant something to him, was given to the person he felt would appreciate them as he did.

In the meantime, George continued to deteriorate and was losing weight rapidly. The medicine wasn't working and his personality was changing as a result. Without the bone marrow that he needed, if he bumped his arm, it had a tendency to break. The vertebrae in his back started to collapse, and George went from a height of five-feet, eleven inches to five-feet, four inches. Throughout all this pain, George made a valiant effort to maintain his unique sense of humor. He was determined to continue the quality of life he had lived for as long as he was able. His desire for hunting never wavered. Even though it cost him great physical pain, George was always eager to go hunting. Riding in a vehicle on the back roads was extremely trying.

"Do you have to hit every bump in the road?" he would yell at me as I tried to avoid the biggest potholes. He tried going out every weekend, but it was becoming increasingly painful. The last time he went, we couldn't ignore it anymore. George was unable to bear the torture and we ended up taking him home because of the excruciating pain. That was hard on all of us, as George had always been part of our hunting. We had to face the reality that it was a part of his life that could no longer continue. All the good times came flooding into my mind: the camping, fishing, hunting, dinners together, and playing cards. No one could play cards as partners like George and I. We were so irrational, no one could ever figure out what we were up to. Tears stung inside my eyelids. I was about to lose a friend who had become as precious as a brother to me.

One Saturday morning, George came over to the house to have a cup of coffee. We were always there for each other, and this day he needed to talk. His wife, Mary Ann, wanted him to take a trip to London with her. I encouraged George to try to take the trip, as I was convinced this would be his last trip anywhere.

"I'm in such pain, LeRoy, that I don't see how I can possibly go. I'll just spoil the trip for Mary Ann," George said. "It hurts to walk and I can't see me sitting that long. I want to do it for Mary Ann, but I don't see any way I can manage it." We changed subjects, as there didn't seem to be any solution to the problem. I started talking about the statue and mentioned to George how I had prayed to Mary and the plan for the face just came flooding in. George wasn't Catholic, but he did believe in the Lady.

"LeRoy, I should have you put a good word in for me," George suggested. I don't know why I did what I did, because it was totally out of character for me, but I stood up and put my hands carefully on George's stooped-over shoulders.

"Mary, please heal my friend, George," I prayed. That was the second prayer I ever made to her. I was as surprised as George was by my actions. I could tell by my wife's face that she was amazed by the whole episode.

"George, I'll go to Mass this afternoon and ask her again," I said, still confused by what I had done.

That afternoon, Pat and I sat in the same seat we had before and I looked up at the statue of Mary and Baby Jesus. I implored her to please ask her Son, Jesus, to heal my friend George.

The next Saturday, the phone rang again. It was George.

"How about a cup of coffee?" he said.

"Sure, come on over," I answered puzzled. George had never called to come over before. He just showed up.

"Who was that?" Pat asked.

"George," I replied. "He's coming over because he has something to tell us."

"Did he say what?" Pat asked.

"No, we'll just have to wait until he gets here, I guess," I said.

When George arrived, he looked like a bubble about to burst. An enormous grin covered his face.

"O.K., George, what is it? You look like you're about to explode," I said, with a funny feeling creeping into my mind.

"Wednesday I went down to Missoula and had a bone marrow test done. It was the first time it hurt. Friday, the doctor called and told me I wasn't going to believe what he was about to tell me. He said the atypical cells had disappeared. He had consulted with other doctors and they couldn't explain the reason either. They want to send me to a clinic in Arizona to see what happened. They are convinced the medicines I've been taking couldn't have worked that fast. I refused to go to Arizona, because I know what happened. My cancer is gone, LeRoy! All day yesterday all I could think of was MY CANCER IS GONE! MY CANCER IS GONE!" George exclaimed, excitedly.

Pat and I just sat there dumbfounded. We couldn't believe what George was saying. The feeling that came over me was indescribable. I felt I was in another world and George was talking miles away. Then it hit me! Mary and Jesus did show me how to build the statue, and to make sure I knew it, He cured George. The only thing that came to my mind then was, "Thank you, God!" I looked at George and kept repeating, "I can't believe it!"

"It could only be one thing --- Our Lady," George insisted.

I was now convinced that miracles do happen. In fact, when I told Ron at work one day, I was able to finally give credit to the Lady for showing me how to build her. I never was fully convinced that it was only my talents that built her, but now after George, I was able to verbalize what had happened to me. I was content to let Ron think I had planned the face structure by myself, but I'll never do that again. Now everyone will know that I had the best possible help --- the Lady herself!

Two years later, George went to Washington to a doctor. He took his records with him. The doctor told George that if he hadn't seen his records, he wouldn't believe it. There wasn't a sign of cancer and all his bone marrow is back. It is now 1991 and George drives a three-wheeler, goes hunting, fishing, and does what he used to. His height will never come back due to the deterioration of his backbone, and he will live with back pain because of the vertebrae. But as George's own words will testify, "I am a very fortunate person and I feel that there was a very wonderful happening in my life. The Lord and The Lady heard LeRoy. I thank God for allowing this to happen to me."

CHAPTER THIRTEEN

OUR LADY AT WORK

Every night when Bob O'Bill came to get the fuel for the equipment, he had a young boy with him. Being naturally curious, I asked Bob about him.

"Whose your friend, Bob?" I asked.

"You mean Billy? He lives across the street from me. He wants to be part of the statue. He's been a big help, even though he is only fourteen. Billy and I pick up the truck and fuel, then we meet Al Beavis and Mike Cerise on the mountain. We've all taken Billy under our wing. Al's even teaching him how to blast on the mountain. Little Billy Fisher is our good luck charm," Bob proudly explained. One day Billy wandered into the shop .

"Hi, LeRoy!" e shouted. "Do you have anything I can do to help?"

"Sure, Billy," I answered, always glad for an extra pair of hands. "Grab those two pairs of vise grips and when I hold these plates together, snap them on the sheet." Billy looked around until he found them. Grabbing them, he quickly came over to where I was holding the iron together.

"O.K., do it!" I told him. He did it, all right. Right on my thumb!

"Unsnap them!" I yelled, in great pain. "Unsnap them! Hurry up!" Quickly, Billy reacted and jumped to unsnap them. Blood poured out of my throbbing thumb. I danced up and down on the floor, first with my thumb in my mouth, then shaking it from side to side.

"I'm sorry! I'm sorry, LeRoy!" Billy kept repeating over and over. Poor Billy e only tried to help. Ron was laughing so hard he was rolling on the floor. At first it hurt so bad, I couldn't laugh, but then the humor of it struck me and I started to laugh, too.

"Billy, does my thumb look like a sheet of iron?" I joked with him when things calmed down. We have never let Billy forget the incident, even to this day. He may be Bob's good luck charm, but he can stay away from me with those vise grips!

Bob laughed when I told him about the vise grips and Billy.

"Thank God for Billy, though," Bob remarked. "When we were on the mountain putting in holes for the power poles, I could always depend on Billy being there, even when no one else was available. We had to dig all the holes by hand, and it's nothing but rock. Sometimes it took a day or more to put in one hole. I've never seen a fourteen-year-old that likes to work so hard, but I'm awfully glad he does."

One day while I was visiting with Ron Hughes in Anaconda, I stopped in to see a friend, Don Keele, with whom I had worked at the smelter and on the pipeline at Georgetown Lake. He inquired about my activities concerning work.

"I'm building that ninety-foot statue in Butte, Don," I related.

"Sure, you are, LeRoy," Don laughed.

"Haven't you heard about it?" I questioned, rather surprised that he might not have.

"Sure, I've heard about it, but you're not the one building it. Someone else is. I remember reading about him in the newspaper," Don replied. It took a lot of convincing him otherwise, but finally he decided to believe me. For the next hour or so, I told him about the progress I had made and what my next plans were. I told him about Ron Hughes living several houses down the road from him, how he came to be there, and how we needed more help. Trying to convince Don to come to Butte and help with the welding was unsuccessful, as he had too much to do as it was. Being an excellent welder himself, Don was greatly interested in the size of iron.

"How are you cutting all that iron, LeRoy?" Don asked.

"With a torch," I replied.

"Why don't you use a gibbler?" Don asked. "That would be so much easier and quicker."

"We've looked, but we can't find one," I said.

"Consider yourself lucky, LeRoy," Don quipped. "I just happen to have one!" We went out to his garage and he showed me what he had. I couldn't believe how big it was. I never knew they built one that size. "If you want to use it, you can," Don offered.

"Thanks, Don," I said gratefully. Don has been one of the most generous friends I have ever known. No matter what I have ever asked him for, he has not only given of his tools, but he has given freely of his time, as well. He has always been this way, from the time I've known him until the present. He's generous to a fault.

Like a new kid with a toy, I couldn't wait to show Ron how the gibbler worked. I placed a sheet of iron on the table and made a cut.

What a find! It cut the iron like a hot knife in butter! When Roberts came in, I couldn't wait to demonstrate how the gibbler worked.

"Watch this, Joe," I said, as I bent over the iron. " This is going to save hundreds of dollars in oxygen and acetylene" Again, it cut the iron beautifully. Joe was impressed.

"I'll be sure to send him a thank-you card from the Lady," Joe exclaimed. He did, and to this day, Don has kept that card as a prized possession.

We completed the shoulders, and needed to remove them from the welding shop to construct the back of the head onto the face. Just as we had described the removal of the shoulders to Joe earlier, we put pipe under the structure and rolled them out into the yard. Then we picked them up with the Hyster and carried them to the paint shop. Our next move consisted of bringing the face into the welding shop and situating the back of the head onto it. It fit beautifully. In order to be able to lift the head and move it from place to place, it was necessary to weld an eye bolt on the very top of her head. Concerned with the weight the bolt would have to contend with, Ron and I made doubly sure of the strength of the welds used to fasten the eye bolt.

Even though we had been fortunate in finding what we needed for the statue, one thing more was still needed: a set of rolls for bending the iron. I had noticed a set of rolls advertised in the local newspaper and approached Roberts with the idea of looking into it. He authorized me to place the call. The rolls turned out to be extremely overpriced. Reluctantly, I reported the price to Joe, only to have him respond with asking the man to donate them. This man really had faith, but I knew the man was firm in his price and would not be open to donating them.

A few days later, Roberts asked me to look at a set of rolls that Four Mile Welding possessed. Eagerly I set out, but was disappointed because they were too small for what we needed. Then we were given the information that Butte Machinery was in possession of a set of rolls. Without too much hope, I set out to evaluate them. They were five-feet long, homemade, and just what we needed. The best part was they would be donated. We took them and placed them in the paint shop which was the only place with room for them. What a help they were after all this time of bending the iron over the table by hand! Mary was still supplying what we needed. I just wish she hadn't taken so long!

We had to move the shoulders out of the paint shop in order to accommodate the set of rolls. We decided to put the head on the shoulders to see how it looked. All winter long we had been building parts. Now came the time to check if they would fit. Ron was a little worried, but I wasn't. I knew Mary was in charge of directing this project., so I knew everything was in good hands. Dave Barker worked the crane, lifting each piece up in place, while Ron and I matched the pieces and welded them in place. The next few days were busy bringing piece after piece from the paint shop. Everything fit with precision, and the pieces had never been together before. Mary did a great job in designing each piece. We were all amazed how huge she looked twenty-seven feet high. We situated the veil and when Ron finished the welds on it, we worked on the hair, bringing it down to the shoulders. Every day Joe would come out and smile. He was proud of the accomplishments and his smile grew larger every time he saw Our Lady.

Head and shoulders of Our Lady

CHAPTER FOURTEEN

"..IF YOU KNEW ALL THAT HAPPENED.."

I could tell Bob O'Bill was pleased with the progress the Lady was making. He would come down almost every evening to check on how she looked. One day as I was getting off work, Bob stopped for an update on the next phase. We sat on the steps and during the ensuing conversation, many thoughts were expressed.

"Bob, I know you got into this project because of your wife and the promise you made, but I can't believe you can be as dedicated as you are," I said, really wanting to know this man better.

Bob didn't say anything, just looked at me. Then in a soft voice, he said, "LeRoy, if you knew all that happened on the mountain since we started this project, you'd know why."

"Bob," I said, "that's what I'm asking you to do, share with me what's going on. Look what happened with me when I asked her for help building the face. And then there's George. I really want to know what is going on with the whole project. Tell me, Bob."

Thinking for a moment, Bob quietly got his thoughts together, then slowly started speaking.

It all started when Joyce was ill in 1979. I was worried sick about her and shared my feelings with a good friend, Dan Ramirez. We were both working for the Anaconda Company in the Berkeley Pit at the time. Dan was quite religious and told me the story of the Holy Mary of Guadalupe. Mary had appeared to a poor Indian named Juan Diego as he was walking home. She told Juan to ask the bishop to build a shrine of her on the spot where she appeared. The bishop didn't take him seriously. Three days passed and our Lady appeared again. Juan explained that the Bishop didn't believe him. Mary sent a sign to prove her appearance, a picture of herself on Juan's cloak. Mary told him she was the Holy Mary of Guadalupe. Then Dan told me if I prayed to Holy Mary of Guadalupe, she would answer my prayer and help us. I didn't dwell on what he had told me until I was sitting in the hospital right after Christmas. My thoughts were filled with the dread of the possibility of losing Joyce. I was feeling very despondent, when the conversation Dan and I had entered my mind. Right then, I decided to pray to Holy Mary.

"Please Holy Mary, help my wife through this operation," I prayed. "If you do, I'll build a statue of you and put it on the mountains overlooking Butte."

"That was my prayer and why I said what I did is still a mystery to me," Bob related to me. "I know you can't bargain with the Lord or His Mother, but I truly meant what I said. I didn't stop there, though. I also said a multitude of Our Fathers, Hail Marys, and any other prayer I could think of. I prayed and prayed all the time Joyce was in surgery. I just couldn't conceive the idea of living without Joyce. It was totally unacceptable to me, and I would implore any force I could that might help me."

"I know how you feel, Bob," I interrupted him. "I don't know how I could live without Pat, either." Bob continued his story:

"My daughters and I waited in the hospital for hours. Then, at last, the doctors came in and told us the operation was a success. I embraced my daughters, and told them we would have a wonderful New Year. We were ecstatic. We went home to celebrate with the rest of our family and friends.

"How come you picked Saddle Rock, Bob?" I asked. "Wouldn't it have been better down lower, like maybe Timber Butte?" Timber Butte is a foothill situated southwest of the main area near Butte and would have been much more accessible.

"It probably would have, but I just felt that Mary wanted to be on the Continental Divide," Bob explained. "I thought about putting a small five-foot statue on one of the lower foothills near the Divide, but as I kept looking up at Saddle Rock and its beauty, I felt that's where the Lady was supposed to be: on top of the world, for all to see."

"When I told my daughter, Michelle," he continued, "and pointed to the spot, she laughed and asked how I was going to put a statue way up there.

"I'll pack it up if I have to," was my answer.

She laughed and said, "That's a long hike, Dad."

"They all thought I was nuts, though, not just Michelle. I feel strongly that's where she's supposed to be. I know everyone felt I would forget about it in time, but the more the time passed, the stronger I felt about it."

"Well, I hate to tell you this, Bob, but if someone told me he was going to put a statue on a mountain standing eight-thousand, five-hundred feet, I would think the same thing. I'm wondering now how you plan on getting this ninety-foot one up there!" I exclaimed.

"We'll worry about that when the time comes," Bob nonchalantly said. He was a man of great belief and was willing to leave that up to Mary.

Bob continued with his story:

When I returned to work, I asked Danny Ramirez his thoughts about putting a statue on the East Ridge. He looked puzzled at first, but when I told him about the prayer for Joyce's recovery, he was all for it. He said the first thing I had better do is find out who owns the land there. I had never given that a thought. Dan figured maybe the Forest Service owned that parcel, so I went up to see Dean Reed, the district manager. After explaining to him what I wanted, he extricated a map showing many mining claims all over the ridge. He showed me where the Forest Service land was located. He instructed me to find someone with a mining claim, and then ask them if I could use their land. Otherwise, I wouldn't have access to the Forest Service land.

My next stop was to the Court House to see Jim Davis in the Treasurer's office. We searched for hours without success, then Jim referred me to the Anaconda Company. They knew more about mining claims than anybody.

I found out after a long search where I wanted to put the statue was on a claim called the Manilla Claim owned by the Ossellos.

"Do you mean the same ones who own the furniture and appliance store here in Butte?" I asked, surprised.

"That's the ones," Bob said, then continued on with his story:

I talked to Guy Sr., and asked if he owned the Manilla Claim on the East Ridge. He acknowledged that he did, indeed, own the claim. When I asked him if he would consider selling it so I could put a statue on it, he informed me he was not the sole owner. His brother in Spokane owned part of it. Guy said he would call his brother and get back to me.

My wife and I have some property in Whitehall, Montana, where we spend a lot of time. Michelle lives next to us and we enjoy the country surroundings.

One day as we were driving over there, Joyce noticed I was troubled. "What's the matter, Bob?" she asked me. "You look pretty toubled by something."

"I don't think the Ossellos are going to let us buy the land for the statue," I replied.

Joyce said, "Look at it this way, Bob. If someone came over here to Whitehall and asked you if you'd sell or donate your property to them to put up a statue, would you give it to them?" I didn't know what to say. I had never thought of it in that light before.

Then Joyce said, "Bob, you made a promise to the Lady because of me. If she wants you to have the land, you'll get it. If you don't get the land, you'll have done everything you could. Leave it to Our Lady now."

I felt better after talking with Joyce. After returning to Butte, Ossello called and reported he and his brother had talked it over and if we were crazy enough to put a statue on Saddle Rock, they'd lease us the land. When I asked him about the surface rights, he told me he was sure they could work something out.

"See, LeRoy, all I had to do was put the whole matter into the Lady's hands," Bob explained as if what had happened was a natural occurrence.

"How did you get all the equipment, Bob?" I said, engrossed in the story completely by now. "Joe Roberts told me you got it from the Anaconda Company. Did they just let you have it or what?"

"Again, that was the work of the Lady," Bob explained. "It has always been hard for me to ask for whatever we need. It seemed like the feeling would have to come to me and when it did, no matter where I was, I felt compelled to do it." Bob continued his story on how he acquired the equipment:

I was down in the change house, when I told a friend, Greg Dundas, that I had to go see Frank Gardner.

"How come?" Greg asked.

"I'm going to ask him about using some equipment to build the road on the mountain," I said.

"You have to be crazy!" Greg shouted. "They just went on a wildcat strike in the Pit. Bob, he won't be in any mood for your request. You'll be lucky if he doesn't toss you out."

"I don't care. It's something I have to do. Will you come along with me?" I said.

"You bet!" Greg replied. "Someone is going to have to catch you when he throws you out. It may as well be me."

"Thanks a lot, Greg," I said ruefully.

When I went in, Frank asked me how I was and asked about Joyce. This led to a proper opening for the reason I had come. I told Frank about Joyce and the promise I had made to the Lady.

After the explanations were made, Frank asked, "What can I do for you, Bob?"

"Frank, we need some equipment," I started slowly.

"What kind of equipment do you have in mind, Bob?" Gardner asked me.

"Well, a Cat D-9, if we could, a grader, and a loader to build the road to the site," I said hopefully.

Frank looked at me curiously. "Are you very religious, Bob?"

I really didn't know how to answer that. I believe in God and His Mother Mary. My mother said the rosary every day and made us go to church. But I hadn't gone to church since I'd been married. I decided to be truthful with Frank.

"No, Frank, I'm not that religious, but I do believe in my faith, and practice it in my own way. I don't go to church as much as I should," I said, wondering what he would think of my answer.

Frank Gardner just sat there listening, and finally he said, "I'm sure we can do something for you, Bob,"

When we left Frank's office, I looked at Greg. He was in a state of shock. "What's wrong with you, Greg?" I inquired.

"I can't believe what I just heard. You ask this man for hundreds of thousands of dollars worth of equipment. He asks you if you're religious, and you say no. He gives you the equipment! I can't believe it!" Greg was astonished.

"Everything seemed to be going great. Then Frank Gardner came down to the Berkeley Pit to see me. He announced he couldn't give me the equipment after all. My heart fell. When I asked the reason, he said I would have to get approval from the Environmental Protection Agency. Because they were not his favorite people, he would be unable to help me. Here was another snag in the plans, but the Lady came to our rescue again. I happened to tell Art Korn about the problems with the EPA. He took care of all the arrangements. By working with Pat Howe from the State Land Board over the telephone for the next six weeks, everything was taken care of. It had been a lot of work, and even Frank Gardner was impressed as to how quickly things had been accomplished."

"How did you get Al Beavis and Mike Cerise involved in the project?" I asked Bob, still enthralled with the happenings.

"Al and I have been friends for a long time and his knowledge of drilling and blasting is what we really needed,"

Bob continued:

Al worked at the Berkeley for years and I just asked him one day if he would help put a statue on the mountain.

"Are you crazy?" Al replied. "Put a statue way up there?"

I told Al about the promise I made and why I wanted to do this. I could tell Al thought it was a crazy idea. I felt I couldn't talk everyone in to this idea, but this is one man I'd love to have.

"Think about it, Al," I said. "You'd be doing something no one else has done." After a few days, I saw Al again.

"I may be as crazy as you, Bob," he stated. "But I'll help."

"What about Mike Cerise?" I questioned Al. "Do you think he'll help, too?"

Al Beavis

"Ask him," said Al. "All he can do is say no." Mike was a shift boss, and a crackerjack heavy equipment operator. He would be just the man we needed to build the road. When I approached Mike, I couldn't believe how easy it was. But then Mike is like that. I don't believe he can say no to anyone. He's just an all-around good guy."

Our next step was to get permission from KXLF to use their road, and persuade them to let us build a road tangent to theirs. After obtaining permission, Al, Mike, and I surveyed the site. We walked the rugged ridge from the TV towers into the saddle of Saddle Rock. I told Al and Mike this was the spot I had picked from my house.

"Do you think this would be a good spot?" I asked looking at the beauty of the surroundings, hoping they would agree.

"You know, Bob, this wouldn't be a very good spot," Beavis exclaimed. "Look at the pile of rocks out in front there," I looked and couldn't see anything wrong with them.

"What's the matter with them. Al?" I said dejectedly.

"Well, if you put a statue here in the saddle, from some parts of the city the rocks would block the view of the statue," Al explained.

"That's right," Mike Cerise agreed. Disappointed as I was, I could see what they meant.

"Well, if we don't put it here, where should we put it?" I asked.

"We'll look around," said Beavis.

Looking at the pile of rocks that were obstructing the view, I decided in a fit of anger to call them "Trouble Rocks" because they were troublesome to my plan.

Each man went off in a different direction. then I heard Mike Cerise holler for Beavis and myself to get over to where he was. On reaching the spot where Mike was, we found him quite excited.

"Let's put it under the rock that looks like a lamb!" Mike said .

"Lamb Rock?" Al and I echoed together. Then Mike pointed to the cliff of rocks. Sure enough, there was a rock sitting on top resembling a lamb.

"That's funny," I said. "We never saw that before. No matter where you stand, you can see it." When we went over and climbed up to the spot where the lamb was, we knew this was to be the location.

"It feels as if we are on top of the world. What a beautiful view from here. Look at all the mountain ranges you can see from here," Al was extremely excited about the spot and couldn't get over the breathtaking view.

"What do you think, Mike?" I asked.

"Great spot!" Mike answered, also taken in by the beauty of it.

Bob paused in his storytelling to remember once again, the thrill of finding Lamb Rock and how it led them to the home for the site of the statue.

Lamb Rock

"You know, Bob," I said, interrupting his thoughts, "when I went up there the men had a hard hat on the lamb and called it the Boss. I called it the Lamb of God, but then it means the same, I guess. God is the Boss!"

"You had better believe it!" replied Bob.

CHAPTER FIFTEEN

SHARING OF FAITH

In another session of sitting on the steps sharing the stories, Bob returned to the subject of acquiring the equipment.

"In April, I went to see the equipment Frank Gardner told me we could have. I was referred to Arnie Harris about seeing which kind was available. Since he was the expert, I let him select the "Cat" which would serve our purpose. Afterward, I asked about a loader. He showed me one which was exactly what we needed and promised a grader would be ready for us whenever we requested it. Boy, was I excited! Now we could really get on with building the road."

Joe volunteered anything he had, but he couldn't guarantee how long we could use it. If a buyer came along, he would have to accommodate his request and sell it. This way, we could count on the equipment being there when we needed it," Bob related.

"Bob, I know you told me before that you went down the mountain instead of across it because of the boulders. Didn't the equipment help?" I asked.

"Some of the boulders were as large as the "Cat" and some were even larger. We tried cutting across the mountain. We even walked across to determine which way was feasible. Bob O'Connor kept insisting we should go straight across. If we had been in possession of blasting and drilling equipment, we would have chosen that way. There was no way to cut through those rocks without blasting and drilling equipment. We would have damaged the equipment too badly. We agreed with Mike to descend the mountain instead of crossing it. There weren't as many rocks and our priority was to keep the equipment in working order," Bob answered me.

"Mike Cerise and Bob O'Connor ran the heavy equipment while Al and I kept ahead of them cutting trees. It wasn't difficult to stay ahead of them because some days they were only able to make ten or fifteen feet. Even though it wasn't very far or fast, it was the best we could do under the circumstances," Bob added.

"You know, Bob," I interrupted. "When I was working on the statue, someone asked me what impressed me the most about the project. I didn't even have to think about it. The men on the mountain were the most inspiring force for me. They worked up there every night until dark, many times without going home for dinner. On their days off, they could be found on the mountain from early morning until dark. Even their vacations were spent building the road. They did that, not knowing for sure there would actually be a statue. Now that's FAITH! I can see what I'm doing. It is real for me. I can touch the steel and see it taking form, but those men on the mountain did it all from pure faith."

Construction of the road in its early stages

"Mike Cerise would have his shift changed to afternoons so he could get up and start early in the morning," Bob remarked, agreeing with everything I had said.

"What would have happened if he had gotten hurt when he was there by himself?" I asked.

"There was always someone going up. If it wasn't me, it was Beavis, O'Connor, and once in a while Dundas or Dorr." Bob said.

"Let me tell you about an incident that happened up there, LeRoy," Bob continued.
One day Mike got too close to the edge of the bank. The ground was soft and caused the "Cat" to slide down the hill. When Mike tried to climb the "Cat" back up

the bank, it was steep with a lot of soft sand which prevented him from ascending. I asked him what he was going to do.

"I'll go down and try to come up another way," Mike answered. I decided to stay on the road, confident Mike would be out in no time. All of a sudden, I heard the machine shut down. Concerned, I returned to the edge of the hill and found Mike had become stuck in an underground spring. The more he tried to get out, the deeper the "Cat" would go. After talking it over, we decided to put the rocks and downed trees under the track of the "Cat." Mike jacked up the "Cat" with the blade and ripper, hoping the "Cat" would climb up the logs and rocks and pull itself out. All efforts failed, and Mike finally suggested we borrow another "Cat" to pull this one out.

"Gosh, Mike," I said, "that means we'd have to go back to Butte, pay to have a truck and lowboy haul the "Cat," and pay a driver besides. Do you know what that would cost? Try again, Mike."

"Bob, even if I get out of this mud hole, it's steeper here than where I first went down," Mike complained.

"Try it, Mike," I insisted.

"O.K.," Mike decided to humor me. We put more logs under the "Cat," then Mike climbed back onto the machine.

"Mary, we need your help if we are to get out of here," I prayed silently to myself. "There's no money to bring another "Cat" up here. We have just enough for fuel. We're doing all this for you." Mike started the machine and it moved a few inches.

"It's coming!" Mike shouted. He repeated the action again and again, and finally it sucked out of the mud hole and climbed the hill to the road. I ran over to Mike.

"I can't believe you got it out of there!" I exclaimed, patting Mike on the back.

"I can't believe it came up this hill," Mike said wonderingly. "It seemed like it had more power than it ever had!"

I looked at Mike shyly and whispered, "I said a prayer to our Lady, Mike."

"I did, too," Mike grinned back at me. "She sure works when you ask her to."

Bob stopped for a minute, thinking of the story he had just related to me. After a while, he continued with his memories.

"We kept going. Some days it was ten feet, other days we made two or three hundred yards. Poor Bobby O'Connor! It was a good thing he was a crackerjack of a machinist, as he was always working on the machinery. Because of the altitude, the "Cat" would overheat continually. That was the Lady's way of telling us to take a break. We would have to wait for the machine to cool down, and that made progress very slow sometimes."

"I saw you take Billy Fisher with you at times, Bob," I said. "Did you ever let him drive the Cat?"

"I showed him how to run the loader," Bob replied. "It wasn't only Billy up there, though. Beavis's son, Toby, Mike's son, Rick, and Billy's cousin, Shane Lewis were up there helping, too. Those boys were all under fourteen-years old, and before they did anything up there, Cerise made sure they knew and understood the safety rules. They were all good workers. They'd cut and haul trees, keep things clean, and whatever we needed, they did. But sometimes they were hard to find because when you get boys that age, they like to fool around." Bob chuckled as he recalled the antics of the boys.

"What really surprises me, Bob, is no one ever got hurt up on the mountain," I stated.

"We were lucky, LeRoy," Bob recalled an incident with Bob O'Connor. "Bob had a close call on the "Cat" one day. He lost his brakes and became entangled in a rock slide. He slid about one hundred feet down a hill. His cool head and experience paid off. That's one reason we never let the kids on the "Cat." It was too big and we needed an experienced operator on the mountain."

"One thing I could never understand is why you had seven switchbacks in the road, but went straight up the mountain instead of a more gradual incline," I wondered out loud.

"We didn't realize we were as close to Forest Service land as we were, but when we did, we went straight up the mountain from then on. It was a good thing we did as it would have taken months to obtain easement rights," Bob-remarked.

"I remember Joe Roberts telling us that when you got to the top, you were going to fire some flares around nine o'clock. He was quite excited and told us to be sure to watch for it. A lot of people had expressed the opinion you would never make it to the top, and this display would show them all," I said.

"I was told that at the Pit, too," Bob said.

"I never did see the flares, Bob," I replied. "I watched for them, but then I live at the base of the mountain, so I may have been too close."

"You missed a big celebration," exclaimed Bob. "We felt like mountain climbers. We had conquered a mountain! We set off some railroad flares, and turned the lights of the "Cat" on. We had some pop and beer donated by Bob Koprivica and Don Harrington. It was like drinking champagne to us. That was exhilarating!"

"I knew the pop and beer were donated because I had to go over once a week and pick them up. How did you get them to donate so much, Bob?" I asked.

"I just went to Bob and Joe's Wholesale and told Koprivica about the project. That's when he tried again to get me to put a cross on the hill instead of Mary. When he saw I wouldn't change my mind, he told me he hoped I'd accomplish my dream. He also promised to provide us with all the beer we needed for the thirsty workers," Bob related. "Thinking I had a good thing going, I went to see Don Harrington at Harrington Pepsi and explained what we were doing. I asked if we could buy pop for the workers. Instead he donated all the pop we needed."

"I can't believe the people of Butte, Bob," I said. "Whatever you need, they seem to be extremely generous."

"Speaking about people donating, LeRoy," Bob O'Bill continued, "so many people haven't even been recognized. We had Al Beavis and his expertise in drilling and blasting, but if it weren't for LaVelle donating his air track drill, large compressor, jacklegs, primers, dynamite, power caps, and primer cord, we would have never been able to move the huge rocks and boulders. This enabled the "Cat" to push them over the side. Al also taught others how to blast for the times he wouldn't be there. Even the young boys knew how to blast, but everyone had to follow the safety rules, or they wouldn't be there."

"Isn't it funny, Bob," I countered, "whatever we need, it seems to be there when we need it. It seems the Lady has each of us picked out for what we know. What about Bill Barth, Bob? How did you find him?"

"I didn't," chuckled Bob, "Mary did."

"How did she do that?" I asked, totally interested. Bob continued with another story:

When we were working on the road one evening, it was time to come home. We worked until dark and were quite fatigued. Coming down the mountain road, I became depressed. It just wasn't progressing as well as it should have. We didn't have enough help. Roberts kept telling everyone about all the volunteers we had. But there was just a handful of us. It wasn't only the help, but the money needed to continue in the way we had planned. Thoughts kept creeping in as I winded down the mountain road. I began to question whether there would ever be a statue on the mountain. Even after all the long hours the crew had put in on weekends and evenings, nothing seemed to be going right. I wondered if it were all for nothing. When I got home, I was too tired to eat or take a shower. I went straight to bed because I knew I had a tough day at work in the morning.

The next morning I mentioned to Joyce what a strange dream I had.

"What kind of a dream, Bob?" Joyce asked.

"I dreamed the Lady came to me and told me not to worry. I would have help. Then I saw this number 505. I wonder what it means?" I wondered out loud. Joyce reassured me that the dream probably meant the statue would be on the mountain and help was on the way. It did make me feel better.

In the Pit, all the trucks were numbered, so as I drove around to different jobs, I kept looking for 505. I really thought it meant something. When we went back on the mountain that night after work, I did feel a lot better and things went smoother. The next day at work, I was called to the pipe tailings to do some electrical work. As I drove up, I noticed a pickup parked there. I couldn't believe it! On the side of the truck was the number 505. Excitedly I walked over to the truck. Bill Barth, a construction foreman, was the driver.

"How's it going, Bill?" I went up to him to start a conversation.

"Great! I heard you were on your way up here from the radio, Bob," Bill answered in return. "How's it going on the mountain?"

"Slow," I remarked.

"I heard Beavis, O'Connor, and Cerise are working with you," Bill stated.

I couldn't hold it back any longer. I had to say something. I jumped right in with it. "Bill, I had a dream the other night, and you're supposed to help us with the statue." I could see Bill was caught off guard and didn't know what to say.

Finally, Bill said, "Are you sure it's me you're talking about?"

"I saw the number on your truck - 505," Bob insisted.

"This isn't my truck. Mine is in the shop for repairs. I've been using this one until mine gets out," Bill said, feeling a little foolish. "But I will give you a shift on the mountain when I get the time."

I thought to myself, "Why did I do that?" But deep down I felt this man was supposed to help. As the time passed, I would see Barth and he would confirm that he still planned on coming up to help. This was one time I felt the Lady might have been mistaken. When the site was about completed, I once again saw Barth.

"Say, Bob," Barth started, "I can go up Saturday and give you that shift." It was a long time in coming in my opinion, but his shift turned into one shift after another. He was hooked just like the rest of us. He was just the man we needed because of his engineering and surveying experience.

With this story completed, Bob stood up and stretched.

"I'd better let you get on home, LeRoy," Bob said. "Our wives are going to wonder what's keeping us." I thanked Bob for sharing with me and told him how much I had enjoyed listening to his stories. When I got home, I wrote down everything Bob had shared with me. I expressed my feeling about how proud I was to be part of all this.

CHAPTER SIXTEEN

KEEPING NOTES

Ron Hughes and I had the head and shoulders about done in April. Joe Roberts asked if we would work the weekend to finish the minor things enabling the statue to be placed in front of the yard for Easter. George James' son, a painter, planned on painting the statue this weekend. The paint had been donated by DuPont. Joe Roberts and Bob O'Bill had spent hours on the telephone convincing DuPont to donate the special paint, which was advertised to last for twenty years at a cost of one hundred dollars per gallon. Joe Roberts had convinced the DuPont Company to donate the paint as an experiment to prove how durable the paint was.

After Ron and I completed the minor welding on the project, we left it to the painter for the rest of the weekend. Monday morning I could hardly wait to view the final results. As I stood looking at the beauty of the statue, I was overwhelmed. She was breathtaking in her gleaming white coat of paint. Joe and I were impressed.

"Get her out in front!" Joe exclaimed. Jim Gilman donated his crane and operator to lift and move the statue to the front of the shop. I stood there, thoughts running rampant through my head. First the hand, then the face, and now the head and shoulders. This really was a dream coming true.

Again, people flocked to see the head and shoulders. Donations again flowed into the box. Among those coming to view the statue were several priests and a nun. I was in the yard working when I spotted them. They were from my parish - St. Anns. I talked to them about the statue, and expressed the different thoughts I had about the rest of the statue. Sister Mary Jo McDonald listened intently to my conversation. I could see she had something on her mind.

"LeRoy, do you keep track of what you do?" she asked.
"What do you mean, track of everything?" I queried.
"Write down what you do every day," she continued.
"Why would I want to do that?" I asked, puzzled.

"Some day in the future people are going to want to know how the statue was built, your thoughts when building it, and some of the special things that happened," she insisted.

"I really don't like to write," I informed her. "My English isn't that great and I'm not much of a speller."

"Put it on tape," she said. "You really should do it, LeRoy."

When I went home that night I told Pat what Sister had said. Pat agreed that it would be a good idea. In fact, she found the tape recorder that evening. After dinner, I retired to my easy chair to sit and watch the news or fall asleep, which ever came first. Pat plunked the tape recorder in my lap and said it was as good a time to start as any.

I started talking into the recorder, feeling extremely uncomfortable the whole time. My thoughts came slow and haltingly. This came as a surprise, as I usually could not shut up if I was talking to someone about the Lady. I was too conscious of the dumb machine sitting in my lap. I tried talking when it was on the table, and even on the floor, but the results were the same. When I played the tape back, I sounded like a robot. The next night, I brought my paper and pen into the room and began writing. I was convinced of the idea of keeping notes, but I would have to overcome my adversity towards English and spelling if this were to succeed. From that time on, I kept a day-by-day diary. Now that I have decided to write this book, I have thanked Sister Mary Jo McDonald many times for persuading me to keep those notes. She had told me I would forget dates, when people came on the project, what they did, and special little things that should be included in the story. She was right. In looking over my diary, I found many little things that at the time seemed to be unforgettable, but in time, they have been pushed aside for other memories. Just going back over them was a special treat for me.

When the statue was out in front, KXLF, the local TV station, came down and interviewed Joe. Many pictures were taken of the head and shoulders. One of the questions asked was how the name "Our Lady of the Rockies" was chosen. Joe Roberts said everyone always called her "Our Lady", but one day Joe and Bob O'Bill decided an official name should be chosen. After some thought, Joe Roberts came up with the designation, "Our Lady of the Rockies". Bob really liked that, but still continues to call her "Our Lady", as the majority of the guys still call her.

Another question came up. "Why doesn't the Lady smile?" Joe was at a loss at first, because it sounded like a good idea to him, too.

The next day Joe came down to the welding shop and asked the same question to me.

"Remember how hard of a time I had building the mouth? What you see is what you get because that's how the Lady wanted to look." I replied to his question.

After some of the excitement had died down from the head and shoulders being in front, Ron and I began work on the next section. While working, Ron's eyeglasses broke. I didn't realize how bad his eyesight was until then. He was almost blind without glasses. When he welded, he couldn't see well enough to find the seams of the plates. I remembered a pair of glasses someone had left at my home. I brought them back that afternoon after lunch and gave them to Ron.

"How do those work, Ron?" I asked anxiously. I hoped they would work, because Ron couldn't afford to buy a pair.

"Better than nothing, but not too good," Ron squinted at me. Having been to the eye doctor for an examination not long ago, I recalled how congenial the doctor had been. Not known for being a shy person, I thought I would talk to the doctor about Ron and see if there was anything he could do or suggest. When Roberts came into the shop, I got him aside for a minute.

"Joe, Ron broke his glasses and is blind without them. I was going to ask the eye doctor if he would donate a pair. If not, maybe he would give the glasses to us at cost, but Ron doesn't have any money to pay for a pair," I whispered to Joe.

"What if they won't donate them?" Joe asked.

"I was hoping we could take the money from the donations to the Lady," I suggested, watching for Joe's expression.

"Go ahead and see what you can do," Joe replied grinning.

I went and talked to Fred Thomas, an optometrist. I related Ron's story to him and his connection to the Lady. Dr. Thomas told me to bring Ron in. Ron went, had his eyes checked, and had a new pair of glasses made. When the time came to pick them up, I asked Dr. Thomas the amount.

"It's a donation to Our Lady," he volunteered. I thanked him and went on my way thinking what beautiful people we have in Butte. Ron thought he died and went to heaven. He couldn't believe how well he could see.

"You know, LeRoy, these new ones are twice as good as the pair I broke. I can see great now!" Ron was elated.

When I came home, Pat always asked what part of the Lady I was working on. I waited patiently for her to ask one day, and right on cue she said, "What are you working on now?"

Grinning from ear-to-ear, I answered her, "I just put a thirty-four bust on our Lady." I waited for her response.

"That's my size!" she blurted out.

"I know, it was the only size I could compare with," I chuckled out loud. We had many laughs over that part of the statue's anatomy. So did the whole shop.

CHAPTER SEVENTEEN

WHAT THE LADY WANTS, THE LADY GETS

At a Chamber of Commerce meeting, the matter of bringing tourists into Butte came up. Joe Roberts kept coming up with using the statue to bring tourists to the area. Finally, the committee took Joe's advice and decided to hold a dinner to raise money for building the statue. Wayne Paffhausen, co-owner of the Copper King Inn, suggested the Inn because of its capacity to hold at least eight hundred people. The only problem they might encounter would be the date, as spring was the beginning of the convention season.

After the date of May 11 was decided on, Joe Roberts was chosen to confer with the head cook and see if that date was open. At first the cook was certain that all of April and May were booked solid, but when she looked in her appointment book, she was shocked. The only day open was May 11! What the Lady wants, the Lady gets!

A few days later, Joe invited Pat and me to the dinner to make sure we would be there. The tickets cost fifteen dollars, with the Copper King Inn wanting nine dollars and fifty cents for each meal, plus a ten percent tip for the waiters and waitress.

"Joe," I said, "do you think it will be worth the time and effort for the amount you will actually make?"

"Not really," Joe agreed, "but the tickets are already ordered.; Besides, it will be good exposure for the Lady. We need to generate a lot of interest in her to keep the donations coming in."

On the day of the dinner, several of the guys told me I was scheduled to give a talk. I knew they were teasing me, but the idea of the remotest chance of speaking scared the daylights out of me. Just thinking about it made me nervous. A speaker I'm not! Pat reassured me all day that if they had wanted me to talk, they would have told me by now. The tone of the teasing from the fellows at the shop stayed with me all day, though. I sure hoped they didn't have something planned to get even for all the times I had played practical jokes on them.

When we got to the dinner, we were surprised to see about seven hundred fifty people or more. What a turnout! People really did want to see that statue on the mountain, and their overwhelming support for this dinner proved it. Pat and I found seats with our friends, and were having a great time. Then Joe Roberts informed us we were expected to sit in the reserved seats at the head table. Reluctantly, we took our seats at the head table, only to find to our dismay that Bob and Joyce O'Bill had refused to sit there. Although we were uncomfortable eating in front of all those people, we did have a beautiful dinner and the company surrounding us made us feel very welcome, indeed.

The entertainment was excellent. Mike Early sang "Ave Maria", Donna Larson sang "On This Day, Oh Beautiful Mother", then Donna recited a poem she had written just for the occasion. It was called "Pilgrimage", and had a great deal of insight to it. Many people had tears in their eyes during the program. The singing and poem touched many people that evening. Joe Roberts, an experienced speaker, gave an excellent talk on what The Lady meant to him. He thanked Bob and Joyce for sharing their promise with him and everyone in Butte. Joe also mentioned my part in building the statue, making me very proud. It was nice to be recognized for the talent the Lady had given me. Joe then asked Bob O'Bill if he had anything he would like to say. Being a shy individual, Bob declined. For one shaky moment, I thought Joe was going to ask me. Relief flooded through me when I realized it was over.

Then my buddies from the shop stood up and shouted, "Speech, LeRoy!" "Speech, LeRoy!" I could have died. I prayed the ground would open up and swallow me right where I stood. I shook my head no, but they continued with their shouting and started to clap their hands, getting the whole crowd into it. Fear raced through me, my heart started to pound furiously, and my mouth felt like cotton. Somehow, I managed to struggle to my rubbery knees, and proceeded to thank everyone: my friends, Roberts, Bob O'Bill, and everyone who worked on the project. I don't recall a word I said. I must have blanked out completely. Pat told me afterwards that I did a great job. I felt better after she told me that. It would have been nice to know what I had said as I said it though. Everyone felt the people were filled with the Holy Spirit. The ones who were touched the most were the young people who waited on us all evening. They gathered in front of the room and donated the ten percent tip they had been promised to Our Lady. It was very impressive and the seven hundred and fifty people gave them a standing ovation.

A few days after the dinner, I was still thinking about the poem Donna Larson had written. I just couldn't get it out of my mind, so I decided to call Donna.

"Donna, this is LeRoy Lee," I started out. "I was so touched by your poem that I wondered if I might have a copy of it?"

"It would be my honor, LeRoy," Donna replied. "I planned on giving you and Joe a copy any way. I'll stop over later."

When Donna showed up, she came into the welding shop. We went out to the head and shoulders, so I could explain what I had done, and what was left to do. During the conversation, I shared with her the stories that had happened up to now.

"Donna, I know the stories are hard to believe," I stated.

"Not to me, LeRoy. I believe because something happened to me, too," Donna responded.

"What happened to you, Donna?" I asked hoping she would share her story with me.

"In the spring of 1984," Donna started slowly, recalling her heartache, "I suddenly lost my husband of thirty-one years to a massive coronary. I was in a state of shock and disbelief when Joe Roberts called and asked me if I would sing at a fund raising dinner for Our Lady of the Rockies. I told him I honestly didn't think I had the strength nor the courage because of just losing my husband. A few days before the dinner, I felt an unexplained need to see the work that had been done. I drove down to Roberts' yard where the head and shoulders were being displayed. As I walked in front of our Lady, I was swept up in awe as I marveled at the immense size and beauty of the work. To think human hands could fashion such delicate work in steel was overwhelming to me. I felt as tiny as a mustard seed and so very insignificant. The sun was gently and warmly shining on her lovely face and on her garments flowing gracefully from her stately shoulders. As I touched her garment, LeRoy, the sun had warmed the steel, and as I brought my hand down the fold of her veil, it turned to a fine white satin. I could feel a holy presence and I dropped to my knees and said a prayer. I knew that it was meant for me to make the pilgrimage. The strength had been granted for a reason and the words of the poem came flowing freely. I rushed to my car, wrote the words and the feelings which had overcome me."

"Donna, had you ever written a poem before?" I asked.

"No," she stated. "That's why when I was driving home, I decided the poem was much too personal to share. But when I got home, I knew I had the strength to sing at the dinner and it was meant for me to do. I had to call him. When I did, and told him I wanted to sing, he was delighted. We chose a couple of songs for the occasion. The night of the benefit dinner came. I was prepared to sing a spiritual ballad. As I rushed to the benefit that night, my folder with my music fell from the car seat. When I picked it up, out fell my hand-written poem. I didn't even know I had it with me. When I arrived at the Copper King Inn, something pushed me into asking Joe if I could read my poem at the dinner. He glanced at it quickly and said sure. So, LeRoy, I stood before hundreds of people, sang my song of praise, and read my poem that I thought was too personal to share. That's why I believe the stories you told. Because it goes to prove that the Lord does, indeed, work in mysterious ways."

"The Lord has touched each one of us for what he wants us to do. He wants to put a statue of His Mother on the mountain. Of this I'm certain," I exclaimed, thrilled that Donna had shared this incredible story with me.

I took Donna's poem home for Pat to read it. Amazement came over her. "This even tells when the statue will be put on the mountain, LeRoy. This will be interesting to see how that comes about. What a beautiful poem!" Pat exclaimed.

I sat there reading it over and over. I felt very close to Donna and the experience she had had in order to write it.

PILGRIMAGE

I paid a visit to Our Lady of the Rockies this Wednesday afternoon.
Although it felt more like a pilgrimage.

As I stood looking up at her wonderful face so beautifully formed,
A feeling of humility, awe, and wonder came over me.

To think that human hands could fashion such delicate work in steel.
Standing at the base of her bust, I felt as tiny as a mustard seed and so very insignificant.
I touched the folds of her garment flowing down from her stately shoulders.
The sun had warmed the pure white steel and had given the steel the feeling of a fine white satin garment.
You could feel a holy presence there, and I took a moment to pray.

It was then I knew that Our Lady of the Rockies will not be just an ordinary statue of steel.
But it is the form of the Blessed Mother of God made possible by the thankfulness, prayers and dreams of many human beings.
Designed and fashioned by people.
People of great faith, vision, artistry, hope, and dreams.

A dream that we all pray to God will see it's full fruition by late summer of 1985.
Gracing the top of the Continental Divide of the United States of America.

Our Lady of the Rockies" shining brightly, with her arm and hands outstretched.
Like a candle glowing in the night, giving us all hope for the future of our town, state, nation, and the world.
Helping to lead the way to peace, health, hope, and prosperity to all.

          by Donna Larson

CHAPTER EIGHTEEN

THE RELUCTANT SPEAKERS

One day soon after, Bob O'Bill called me on the telephone. Someone had invited him to give a speech to the Daughters of Isabella.

"LeRoy," he pleaded, "would you please go with me?"

"I don't know, Bob," I said, not really knowing why he had asked me in the first place.

"Please, I really don't want to go by myself," Bob implored.

"What about Joyce?" I asked.

"She won't go," Bob said.

"Well, how about Joe Roberts?" I suggested.

"They want the workers," Bob replied.

"Get Al Beavis, Mike Cerise, or Bob O'Connor," I was starting to get exasperated with him.

"LeRoy, you are the one building it. They want you," Bob insisted.

"Do I have to say anything?" I asked, recalling my fright at the last dinner.

"Probably," Bob hesitantly said.

"I'm not going, Bob. I don't like to talk," I quickly rejected his offer and ended the conversation.

The next day, Bob called again and renewed his efforts in trying to get me to go with him.

"Come on, LeRoy," Bob implored. "Please go, as a favor to me?"

"I told you, Bob, if I have to say anything, I won't go," I was adamant about giving a speech.

"It's me they called first, so I guess I'll have to be the one to talk. Will you come along and give me moral support, LeRoy? I really need someone along," Bob pleaded once more.

"I'll go, Bob, but only to give you support. Remember, I don't have to get up and say anything, now," I answered him.

The night of the dinner rolled around and Bob picked me up in his car. When we arrived, we had to push each other in the door. We were both nervous as we sat at the head table. The only satisfaction I got out of sitting there is they finally had Bob sit at the head table. Looking around, I discovered about one hundred ladies, four priests, and the bishop. After dinner, the bishop gave a talk about donating to the Church. Bob was next on the agenda, and the bishop decided to leave. Bob seemed more relaxed after the bishop left, and started telling about building the road and some of the problems they had encountered. His talk finished, Bob sat down with a great sigh. The Mistress of Ceremonies then looked at me and asked me to say a few words.

    I glared at Bob and said, "Do I have to?"

    "They fed you, didn't they?" Bob smiled at me.

    I walked over to the podium and all I could think about was what name to call them. At home, I kept calling them the Daughters of Jezebel, and Pat had to keep reminding me of Daughters of Isabella. No matter how hard I tried, I couldn't keep the name straight in my mind. So now, not only was I nervous about talking, but I also had to try not to say the wrong name. Oh boy, was I in a spot! My knees were shaking so bad, they were knocking together. Thank God I was able to lean on the podium. I said a quick prayer, and started by saying, "Thank you for having us, and I was proud to be part of Our Lady of the Rockies."

    Thoughts of panic were running through my mind because I didn't have the foggiest idea what to say next. Then the prayer must have taken hold because I decided to share some of the stories that had happened. As soon as I started to talk, my knees stopped shaking. I described how I had asked Mary to help me build her statue, the story about George, Bob getting the land, the Lamb Rock, and the Cat being stuck in the mud.

    Then I started telling about Bob going to see Frank Gardner and asking him for the equipment. When I got to the part about Frank asking Bob if he was very religious, and Bob replying that he hadn't been to church for twenty-five years, one hundred heads turned towards Bob and looked at him.

    "Oh, what had I done?" I thought to myself. "Bob is going to kill me. But then, on second thought, that's what he gets for asking me here." I got a certain satisfaction from that. When I completed my talk, the ladies flocked to us. They had loved hearing the stories. I breathed a sigh of relief because Bob had forgotten about all the ladies looking at him when it was disclosed he hadn't been to church for twenty-five years.

    We needed to bring the head and shoulders back to the welding shop so we could situate the bust on it. Joe was against the idea because the donations were still coming in strong, but he finally consented to do it. Jim Gilman's crane was being used some place else, and Dave Barker thought he could walk the sections down with the fifteen-ton crane in the yard. I had my doubts, as the head was quite heavy. When Dave picked up the head, the wind was blowing, causing the head to swing back and forth and banging into the crane at times. It took some time to walk the structure down, but we did succeed in getting it to the other section. Dave raised the head about seven feet off the ground. I got a rope and secured it to one of the legs. Just as I walked out from under the head, the cable on the crane broke. The head and shoulders crashed to the ground with a booming noise. It hit on the back legs, then surged forward toward the ground. Standing there petrified, we watched with horror as the metal leaned eastward with the face extending towards the dirt. At the last minute, the statue paused, then fell backwards onto the legs. After rocking back and forth in small spurts, the steel finally settled on the ground still upright. I looked at Roberts ashen face and had a good idea what he had been thinking. Thank God she hadn't continued on her downward thrust into the dirt and ruined everything we had accomplished up until then. I also thanked God that I hadn't been under the structure when it had dropped. Still shaken over the whole incident, we investigated to see how much damaged had been caused. Some of the iron in the back had been bent and some bolts had to be replaced, but that wasn't too bad for what it had gone through.

The next day, Joe came down to assess the damage. I reported what had already been accomplished and all that remained was to re-weld a few of the cracked welds.

"They must have been improper welds, to have broken," Joe replied, masking his anxiety about the statue with his gruffness.

"Joe, we had ground down the welds, and for them to have dropped seven feet, we were lucky that only a few of them had cracked," I said defensively, thinking of the pressure that had been applied from the weight of the head and shoulders to the welds.

After Joe left, I looked at Ron apprehensively, as I knew he would be hurt by Joe's remark concerning the welds. I wasn't wrong in assuming Ron would be hurt. He was so angry he was muttering to himself, " I'd like to see his bones after he was dropped seven feet! Bad welds, my foot!"

I had done all the cutting and bending of the iron, and Ron had followed behind, welding the pieces together after I had tacked them in place. Ron was mad the rest of the day, and I felt he was justified in his anger.

Marty Petritz from General Distributing came down once a week selling oxygen, acetylene, and rod. He had watched the progress of the statue from the first finger and was amazed at its growth. Marty had compared the statue to watching a baby being born, and seeing it develop into a full grown lady. Marty would donate something to the statue with every order that was placed. When he found out that she had been damaged, he felt as bad as we did. I guess he considered himself a godfather to the Lady.

Weeks passed, and I kept noticing something different about the statue. Finally I mentioned it to Joe.

"Have you noticed the face of the statue? Ever since we dropped her, she looks mad. Is it my imagination?" I said.

"Yes, I noticed that, too," Joe agreed. "But I thought it was just me. I'm glad you mentioned it; I thought I was seeing things."

After a couple of weeks, the face of the statue appeared to be the same as it was before we dropped her. But just like a lady, she prefers to be treated gently.

Head and shoulders overlooking the main shop in Roberts Yard. Small building on right is the welding shop where statue was built.

CHAPTER NINETEEN

LAMB ROCK

"How's it going on the mountain, Bob?" I said.

"They put in a lot of power poles for the lights while I was on vacation," Bob replied. "Roberts told me that they have been talking about a chair lift to transport the people to the mountain. He mentioned a friend who knows an engineer who might be able to help."

A couple of days later, Joe brought an engineer to the welding shop. He asked me to show him around and explain what had been done. Three sections of the statue had been completed; we had just finished the arm and were putting the belt on. The engineer seemed impressed with what had been done, especially when he realized I hadn't even finished high school.

"This would blow most engineers minds," he said. But I'll tell you one thing right now, if you don't hire a designing construction engineer to design the base for this statue and chair lift, it will never pass by the State of Montana. You'll never be able to bring people up there."

"What would that cost?" I asked him.

"You're probably looking at thousands of dollars," he quickly estimated.

"I don't know where we'd get money like that!" I exclaimed incredulously.

The engineer was looking at the six-inch channel we had extending from the legs to the skin.

"How come you did that?" he asked.

"When we placed the head and shoulders on the next section and bolted it together, we had a one inch gap in front. We tried pulling it up with bolts and using a come-along, but it wouldn't come together. Dave Barker, the crane operator, suggested running channel from the post up to the skin. The straight ones were bending and letting the skin drop. We went and found six-inch channel taken from the Ryan Mine, and welded them on. It worked so well, we continued doing that for all of the sections," I said.

"Was he an engineer?" the engineer asked.

"No, would you believe a transport driver?" I remarked.

The engineer continued to look around at the structure. He seemed to be impressed with the pipes, how they had been built and bolted in the right manner.

"You must have had an engineer to design that," he insisted.

"No, we designed and built it that way," I proudly insisted.

"I can't believe you did that without an engineer. You guys did one heck of a job!" he exclaimed.

"We're planning on building the belt and veil out of screen to relieve the wind pressure," I mentioned to him.

He took another look at the statue, and then came up with his opinion.

"I don't think putting screen in the belt is a good idea. The screen in the veils would be all right, though. In the belt, if the wind hit the statue from the sides, it would put a lot of pressure on it. If the wind blew straight, it would be all right, but you can never depend on the wind blowing straight," he remarked.

Joe's reaction to the price of getting an engineer was the same as mine: complete astonishment. When Bob came down a little later that day, I broke the news to him about the engineer's price.

"Would he be willing to donate?" Bob asked, hoping he would. When he found out otherwise, Bob retorted, "If he doesn't want to volunteer, he can jump in the lake!" I had never heard Bob talk in that manner before, and it was quite a surprise. Although I'm sure Joe felt the same way, he was just quiet about it.

Joe sent Ron and me to the mountain to work on the loader and "Cat". When we arrived, I spotted Bill Barth. Never one to miss a chance to rub it in, I walked over to where Bill was working.

"Bob got you, huh?" I laughed. "I told you when we were pitching horseshoes, that you were supposed to help. But you know, Barth, the Lady wasn't ready for you yet. You were meant to work on the site and get it ready for the base. Bob told me you were coming up every day with crews and working daylight to dark. What are you up to now?"

"You know what Barth wants to do now?" Bob said coming over to join us.

"What?" I asked interestedly.

"He wants to take off twenty feet more on the north side. That means the Lamb will have to go," Bob said.

"It has to go, the ground is too soft to put a base out here. We have to go in twenty more feet," Barth insisted.

"I'm like Bob and the rest of them, Bill. I hate to see the Lamb go, too," I tried to persuade him otherwise.

"It's going," Barth was adamant.

"What about the Lamb?" I asked anxiously. "Can't you put some tires around it, cable it, and let it down?"

" It's not going!" Bob insisted as Barth just glared at him. Leaving those two to settle the matter of the Lamb, Ron and I worked on the machinery we were sent up to weld. Later I went back to talk to Barth. In the conversation, I mentioned the engineer I had talked to and the price that was quoted. Barth thought a moment, then volunteered to talk to a few retired engineers from the Company.

The next day, Bob came into the yard requesting some tires. I started to laugh.

"Barth won, I see," I said jokingly.

"Even Beavis and Mike Cerise tried to talk him out of it," Bob went on to explain. "We put Bill in charge of the construction on the mountain, so if he says it goes, it goes. But we can try and save the Lamb. At least we'll try to. I hope this works."

"When do you expect it to go?" I asked.

"Probably Monday," said Bob.

That weekend my daughter, Kathy, and her husband, Jerry, came up from Denver, Colorado. We decided to go to the mountain. After obtaining the key from Joe Roberts, we took a ride to the site and took pictures of Lamb Rock. My daughter and her husband were quite impressed with all the work that had been done.

Later that week, I saw Bob again.

"How did it go with the Lamb, Bob?" I asked.

"It didn't," Bob replied sadly. "When we blasted, the cable broke. We found the rock, but the head came off so we put it aside hoping that someday we could put it together again for people to see." Everyone felt bad about the Lamb, but it was gone. Poor Barth was on everyone's list. That didn't bother Barth, though.

"What do you want, the statue or Lamb Rock up there?" he would reply every time someone would give him a bad time about the rock. They would stop needling him then, because he was right. You couldn't have them both.

We had put a plate around the top and bottom of each section to reinforce each piece and also installed rings so we could bolt the sections together and take them apart when we needed to. It was time now to bring the middle section down and put the hand section under it.

In the meantime, Bill Barth brought two retired engineers and explained to them what had been done on the statue with the hope that one of them would be touched enough to volunteer to help. After they had investigated thoroughly, they left and Barth came into the shop. He had hopes that Laurien Riehl was interested enough to help with the base. Indications from their conversation seemed to be leaning that way.

"I hope Laurien is interested, as he is one of the top design engineers in his field. If we can get him here, we'd have one of the best," Barth explained.

"I hope he works out better than the last one that was here," I said, not as optimistic as Barth.

"He looked at all the structures and the inside. He especially liked the way they were built with the rings to take them apart when you needed to." Barth reported.

A few days later, Roberts came down to the welding shop.

"It looks like we are in luck. Laurien Riehl wants to help with the foundation of the statue. He also wants to know what kind of wind pressure will be hitting the statue when it's on the mountain." Joe was ecstatic about having an engineer involved.

"I have angle iron out to the skin for that problem," I reported.

"Well, Riehl said that's not enough. It has to push toward the legs of the statue," Joe responded. "Well, one thing for sure, we don't want the statue to come down."

"I'll take all the advice I can get," I said. "Look how helpful Dave Barker was when he suggested we put the channel up so it would hold up the skin. When is Riehl going to do this?" I asked.

"He's working on the wind pressures right now. He wants to see how much wind hits each section," Joe said.

A few days later Riehl and his son came to take measurements. He seemed like a really likable guy.

"I understand Barth talked you into helping with the foundation," I said as I approached him in the yard.

"I've been thinking about a circular one," he said. "It will put less stress on any one segment of the base. It will resemble what I want to do on the statue for wind pressure. I can't believe what you have done without any experience!"

"I didn't do it," I replied. " My help came from upstairs." He laughed. I got the same reaction from other people, so it didn't bother me.

When Riehl completed his figures on wind leverages for each section, he came and showed me there had to be more bracing with the angles pointing in a V-shape, so the pressure would go to the legs. After Riehl left, I told Ron about some boom trusses we had gotten when we tore down the Ryan Mine. We went to the yard to see if they were still there, and sure enough, there they were. If we cut them apart, we'd get four sides out of each truss. That would be enough for each section of the statue. We could weld the angle from leg to leg and then weld the v-angles to the skin. It wasn't the same as Riehl suggested, but would be close, and most important, save buying a lot of iron. Proudly we showed them to Roberts and explained how they would work. The best part was, there was enough of them to complete the whole statue. Again, Mary was at work showing us what we needed when we didn't have the money to buy with.

CHAPTER TWENTY

A PRAYER GROUP ENCOUNTER

"The face you constructed is beautiful!" said a voice. I turned around to see who was talking. There stood a young man with a slight build, dark hair, and wearing a smile from ear-to-ear. At first I was taken back, as I had been so busy working, I hadn't even heard anyone come into the shop.

"My name's Vic Duran," stated the smiling face. "I'd sure like to help on this statue. Is there anything I can do?"

"Can you cut or weld?" I asked him.

"Not really," he answered honestly. "I did take a couple of classes at Vo-Tech, and my father-in-law tried to teach me a little, but I wasn't very good at it. I'd sure like to do something, though."

Grinning at his honest remark, I took an immediate liking to this personable fellow with the black moustache.

"Come on," I said. "I've got just the job for you." I grabbed some cutting glasses and motioned for Vic to follow me. We walked across the yard to where Ron was busy cutting the trusses apart. On seeing us approach, Ron stood up, glad to have a few minutes break.

"I've got a replacement for you, Ron," I joked with him. "Ron, this is Vic Duran. He just walked into the shop telling me he has no welding skills, but he has a strong desire to help with the Lady. What do you think? Shall we let him join us on the chain gang?" Ron was only too happy to relinquish his spot on the trusses.

"Here, Vic," I said as I handed him the cutting torch. Vic looked at it with an odd look on his face. Everything had happened too fast for him. Taking the torch back, I showed him how to use it. I cut a few pieces of iron and then let Vic try.

"Don't worry about it, Vic. If you have any trouble, Ron and I can re-cut it after we get it up above," I tried to reassure him. Vic picked up the torch, and began cutting the best he could.

As Ron and I were walking back to the welding shop, he said, "Where did you find this guy? He can't even light a torch!"

"Hey, you weren't that great when you started," I retorted back. "I remember when I first started, too. Give the guy a chance, Ron. Besides, we need all the help we can get, remember?"

"How much time can he put in?" Ron asked, laughing because he did remember how it was when he started.

"I forgot to ask him," I stated. "I'll ask him when I go down to check on him. Anything will help, though."

Vic Duran

Later, when I went to check on Vic, I noticed he had improved a little in his cutting.

"Catching on to it, I see," I said checking some of his cuts.

"Yeah, but when this blows back, the sparks sure do smart," Vic replied displaying some burn holes.

"They should," I answered. "It's red hot melted iron that you're feeling. Here, let me show you what you're doing wrong. You're holding the torch straight in. Cut at a slight angle and don't hold the torch too close." I showed him again, then handed the torch back to him. After a few minutes, he had it working pretty well.

"Boy, that works great!" he exclaimed happily.

"By the way, Vic, how much time are you going to be able to give?" I questioned him.

"Well, I'm a fireman and I work swing shifts. When I'm working night shift is about the only time I'll be able to come." Vic explained apologetically.

"Hey, we haven't had any help. All you can give will be a big help." I went on, "This way Ron and I can work on the statue. What made you come down in the first place?"

"I came from a large Mexican Catholic family and we're all devoted to Our Lady of Guadalupe. We pray to her all the time. I know anyone who works on the statue will be taken care of by her." Vic answered.

"You should hear how she's already taken care of people, Vic." I started sharing the stories that had happened to everyone since the project had begun. I just love to share when I know the people believe what I'm saying. Vic was like a kid who just received some candy. His mouth was open and his eyes were enlarged as if to take it all in. He was indeed, impressed.

"That's beautiful!" he exclaimed when I finished the sharing. "When I first looked at the statue's face, I knew there was more to this than just a bunch of iron."

Bob O'Bill and I were asked to talk on TV. The reporters from the station came to the shop to interview me, then proceeded to the mountain to interview Bob. I told them how I had help to build the face, and how George had been cured. I used the word miracle a few times. That evening, when our interviews were on the air, I felt they had gone pretty well. The next morning, Joe stormed into the welding shop quite upset. I had worked with Roberts long enough to know when Joe was angry.

"From now on, stay off the radio and TV! Don't talk to anyone any more!" Joe shouted at me, furiously.

"What did I say that upset you so much, Joe?" I asked him.

"Don't you ever use the word "miracle" to any one again! I don't want anyone coming down here thinking that there will be some kind of miracle," Joe ranted and raved on.

"Joe," I interrupted, "the statue is for whatever the people want it to be. A piece of art, if that's what they want, or if they want it as a religious symbol, they should have that right."

"Just stay off TV!" Joe raved on, then stomped out of the welding shop slamming the door.

I looked over at Ron.

"Think he was mad?" I ventured, and shook my head.

"If he wasn't, he sure missed a good chance," Ron said laughing.

That night I saw Bob. He was upset, as Joe had talked to him, too.

"I think I made Joe mad," I started out.

"Don't feel bad," Bob said. "He told me the same thing he told you. From now on if the TV or paper calls, he'll be the one to do all the talking. I didn't want to be on TV in the first place."

"I'm sorry I got you in trouble, Bob," I apologized. "I know it's what I said about miracles that caused it all."

Not long after, I was asked to give a talk at the prayer group held at St. John's. I tried to avoid doing it, as I was still quite nervous about talking in front of people. I let time elapse, but finally, the decision had to be made. The nervousness I had felt at the Daughters of Isabella Dinner kept returning to terrify me. Pat told me to pray on it, but I kept praying against talking instead. The feeling persisted that I was supposed to talk even when the coward within me held me back. The same feeling engulfed me when I had told Bob I would go with him to the talk. I was reluctant, but yet some urging force inside kept tugging at me to go. I felt the Lady had sent me to the Daughters of Isabella to share what she has done on the project. I now felt the same urgings, even though I was thinking of every excuse I could not to go. The man had called inviting me to talk because of the stories I had shared at the dinner. Finally, I gave in to the strong inner feelings and said yes, I would speak. Pat agreed to go with me. Neither of us had ever been to a prayer group meeting before and did not know what to expect. What happened there was totally beyond what we were used to.

The people we encountered at the door were friendly and welcomed us heartily. They made us feel very comfortable. When the time for the program came, everyone gathered together facing the south of the building. Songs of praise filled the basement of the church. We felt the music was beautiful and inspiring. The music slowly faded and people all around us started talking in tongues. This was extremely foreign to us, and we looked at each other in surprise. I leaned over towards Pat and whispered, "Are they Catholic?"

Surprise was written all over Pat's face, and I almost cracked up when I saw her puzzlement. Since she had been a Catholic all her life, I figured she knew what was going on.

"I think they are," she whispered back. "I've seen many of these people in church before." Then the worshippers broke into songs of praise again.

The time had come for my talk, and I slowly advanced towards the podium. But my speech was not to be, --- yet. About twenty people came forward wanting to pray over me before I started. I slumped back down in the chair, and they placed their hands on my head, shoulders, and back. Then they broke into a song of prayer. Feeling strange and uncomfortable, my first thought was to bolt for the stairway and run from there quickly. Too many people stood between me and my escape route, so there I sat, a victim of my own big mouth. I did happen to get a glance at Pat's face, and the same thoughts were mirrored on her face as well. Finally, the agony ended and to my surprise, I felt much better. I was nervous, but not nearly as bad as I had been before. As soon as I started presenting the stories, all sense of nervousness vanished as I realized I was doing the Lady's work. Afterwards, many people came over to discuss the Lady and how they could help. I felt many benefits would come from this talk, and the future proved that it would.

A couple of days later, Ron and I were dispatched to the mountain to complete some welding on the air truck drill and build a hitch on it. Bob O'Bill had told Joe Roberts that if we had time while we were there, the loader had a big crack in the bucket that needed fixing. As the day was sultry, we were glad to be on the cool mountain. We completed the drill and hitch, then drove down to assess the loader. The bucket was upside down and we were unable to locate the key to turn it upright. We decided to weld what we could and repair the rest some other time. We took turns cutting and welding. I welded a large crack on the right side before turning the stinger over to Ron to weld for awhile. I sought out some shade under a pine tree and gulped a big drink of water. As I sat there, I noticed something under the bucket. Curious, I wandered over and peered under the metal. I couldn't believe what I was seeing. There were boxes of dynamite and blasting caps. Beavis had placed them under the bucket so no one would take them. I yelled at Ron.

"You won't believe what's under that bucket," I shouted. "Get out of there, NOW!"

"Oh, my God," Ron moaned when he realized the danger we had been in.

"Our God helped us that time," I stated when we had back away. "I don't know why it didn't go off with all the sparks around it. Someone up there loves us."

When we told Roberts about it, he just shook his head in wonderment.

About a week later, Bob O'Bill reported that someone had gotten under the bucket and removed part of the dynamite. Bob reported the incident to the police. They had Bob escort them to the site. After looking at all the signs on the gates and around the site, they informed Bob we had done all we could to keep people out. The next day, the police called and reported to Bob that a fourteen-year-old boy had taken the dynamite home and in the process of cutting them with a knife, it exploded. Bob was quite upset when he heard about the incident. He was a lucky little fellow. He had only injured an eye and a finger.

"That's all we need," said Bob, "for someone to go up there and get hurt. They don't belong there, they shouldn't be there!" Bob was very upset with the whole incident.

"Bob, you can keep the gate locked, but there is no way you can keep people from hiking up there. You can't feel responsible for everyone that won't read the signs," I tried to reason with him.

"I know," said Bob sadly.

CHAPTER TWENTY ONE

OUR LADY HELPS OUT AGAIN

Bill Barth commenced building the forty-eight foot circular base designed by Laurien Riehl. He called me over to examine the prints.

"What do you think, LeRoy?" Bill asked after I had a chance to glance over them.

"I'm not an engineer, Bill," I replied, "but they look good to me. He did an excellent job, as far as I can see."

"He put a lot of work into it, I can tell you that," Bill remarked. "Laurien said the circular design was necessary because it wouldn't put any one segment on the base under extreme stress even though the wind can blow over one hundred miles per hour during a storm."

"My God, Barth, look at the rebar in that thing! Where in the world are you going to get that much, and how are you going to make it round?" I exclaimed.

"That's what I want to talk to you about," Bill said, amused at my remarks. "Do you think you could heat it with your torch?"

"How long are they?" I asked amazed at the enormity of the job. "And what size?"

"Forty-feet long and three-fourths thick," he replied.

"Barth, you won't live long enough for me to heat that much rebar," I exclaimed. "Look how many are in there. You better find a set of rolls, Bill."

"I tried," he said. "I can't find a set any place."

"What about the Anaconda Company?" I said.

"When I worked there," commented Bill, "they had a set, but once the rebar is rolled, you wouldn't be able to get them out of the building."

"You have a problem, Bill," I remarked shaking my head.

"Well, if we can't find a set, we're going to have to get a lot of cutting outfits and heat the rebar," Bill said, feeling the weight of the problem. He had hoped I would come up with a solution. Bill left to see if someone else could help him.

I noticed one of the carpenters by the forms which were being built for the base. He looked familiar, and when I approached the base, I recognized him as Bill Perusich. I used to run around with his brother when I was younger.

"How did Barth get you on this?" I asked coming up to him.

"You don't say no to Barth," he said. "He hounds you until you say yes." Laughing, I walked back to where I was working, thinking that the Lady had picked Bill Barth for a reason. No one is able to say no to him.

Later that evening, I went to Stodden Park to pitch horseshoes with Barth. As I was waiting to pitch against Bill, I noticed the man Barth was pitching against. He was a big man, with white hair and a bushy white beard. I thought to myself, "He'd make a good Santa Claus." Little did I know that Earl did indeed play the part of Santa to many young children all over Butte every Christmas.

Bill Barth was telling Earl Casagranda about the circular base they were constructing. As I listened to Barth talk to Earl, I had to chuckle. I knew exactly what he was up to. He knew Earl was a Jack-of-all-Trades, and one excellent carpenter. Just as I thought, Bill asked Earl to volunteer his services to the Lady. Earl kept making excuses or ignoring Barth when it came time for an answer. Finally, in desperation to keep Barth off his back, Earl said he would come to help.

Earl is a retired fireman, not by choice. He had been working on a fire when the floor gave way and Earl fell through. After two or three operations on his back, the doctors would not release him to return to his job. Earl had to take an early retirement from the fire department.

When it was my turn to pitch against Earl, I started the conversation by telling him he would enjoy working on the Lady. Earl had his doubts, but he did promise Barth.

Earl remarked that when he first heard of the statue, he had no enthusiasm for it. He wasn't against it, either. He really had no feelings one way or another. After the first shift, Earl was hooked on the statue just like the rest of us. The Lady strikes again!

Not long after, Barth came into the shop with a smile on his face. "LeRoy," he said. "Guess what! We were able to acquire some of the rebar from the Anaconda Company. When we went to purchase it, they donated the rest. How about that? Then I went to the Parrot Mine where they were re-training workers, and talked to Arnie Harris about using the rolls to bend the rebar. Harris couldn't let us use the rolls, since they were being used for the training sessions. Seeing the disappointed looks on our faces, Harris suggested we think about using the set of rolls in the yard, which had been brought over from the

Anaconda Smelter when they had closed down. When Harris took me to look at them, I couldn't believe my eyes. Here was a set of rolls exactly what I was looking for. All I had to do was run an extension out of the Parrot Shop for electricity."

"We don't worry about what we need, Bill," I said. "The Lady takes care of it."

Bill persuaded a couple of retired iron workers, John Shea and Tom Holter, into helping bend the rebar. One day, when John Shea came to put the rebar in the circular base, he related his feelings about Barth to me.

"Barth was one of the toughest bosses I had ever worked for," John went on. "He was always in trouble with the Iron Workers Union because he would do the work himself. He worked as hard as his men, if not harder. He's in his glory, now, because he hasn't any unions to stop him. What a hard taskmaster!"

Butte is a union town, but because the statue is all volunteer work, they leave us alone.

It had taken almost four bent rebars to go around the inside of the circular base. Each piece had been bent at the Parrot machine shop, and then brought down to Roberts. They had to assemble it in the yard so they could match and color code the rebar. That way they would know where each piece belonged when they hauled them to the mountain site.

One of Barth's good friends, Pete Tallon from California, volunteered to help with the base. He was so intrigued by the statue, he extended his trip in order to help with it. He purchased a four wheel drive pickup just to haul the rebar to the top of the mountain. Pete instructed me to build a rack for the truck to accommodate a load of rebar forty feet long, but he needed to get permission from Joe Roberts to do that. Joe was delighted when he told me to build the rack. It turned out Pete had donated the truck to the Lady, when it was no longer needed for the hauling of rebar. Considering that the truck cost thirteen hundred dollars, that was no small donation.

"We have a bunch of Safeway scaffolding over there. If I welded one behind the cab and one on each bumper, you should be able to haul the rebar on it," I told Pete.

"Will you be able to take them off, or would they be permanent?" Pete questioned me.

"I'll weld pipe on the bumpers, and then you can just drop them in, or take them off when you want to," I replied.

In the meantime, Vic Duran, who was still cutting the trusses apart, had improved his cutting skills very quickly. He was exceedingly faithful in showing up when he had the time. I decided to start him welding, because it was tiring just cutting on the trusses. Vic was delighted with the idea. I demonstrated how to run the wire machine and to weld the rings for the statue sections.

"I'm a little worried that I won't do a good job," he stated, knowing how important the welds were to the project.

"Don't worry," I replied, "that's why I'm starting you here, inside the statue. If the welds don't turn out very well, Ron and I can always come and redo them. Running a wire welder is a lot easier than stick welding."

"Boy," Vic said, impressed with the welder, "I can't believe how nice these run." I watched Vic for a while, and seeing he was going to be all right, I left him to enjoy himself.

The next day, Joe had a meeting with Laurien Riehl. Laurien wanted to disassemble the lower four-foot section and take it on the mountain. He intended to drill large rock bolts into the base and install the four-foot section inside the forty-eight foot circular base, then pour concrete around it. When I heard this, I became indignant.

"Do you know what you're saying, Joe?" I asked angrily. "If we do that we'll shorten the statue to eighty-six feet."

"He's the engineer, LeRoy," Joe insisted. "If that's what he wants, then that's what we'll do."

"Joe," I retorted, "I designed the statue for ninety feet. If we take four-feet off, it will look stupid! Joe, you're close to six-feet tall. If you took four inches off your legs, don't you think you would look stupid?" Joe left, and I was greatly agitated. I went and examined my print of the Lady, put a piece of paper up from the bottom to where four feet would be. "Stupid!" I repeated over and over.

When I saw Bob O'Bill, I vented my feelings about taking four feet off the Lady and inserting them into the ground. But I didn't get any satisfaction from Bob, either.

"He's the engineer of the base, LeRoy," Bob went on. "If he says that's what he has to do, then I guess that's what they'll do." I was still upset, and could not be pacified over this.

When Barth came in, I once again voiced my opinion on taking four feet off the Lady. I got a different reaction from Barth.

"I really don't like the idea of rock bolts," Barth said. "What we should do is put holes in the rocks, and fill them with rebar and concrete.

I'll talk to Laurien." I felt a little relieved, but wasn't entirely sure Barth could do anything about the situation.

A few days later, I encountered Barth again. He had talked to Laurien about drilling holes and putting rebar into them. Laurien had been open to the idea and was now considering it seriously to save the four foot section of the statue. I thanked Bill over and over again for interceding for me.

CHAPTER TWENTY TWO

DEVOTION TO MARY PAYS DIVIDENDS

One morning a woman entered the shop and introduced herself as Doris Young. She had been impressed during the prayer group meeting at St. Johns when I had given my talk. While asleep, the Lady entered her thoughts and asked her what she was going to do to help Our Lady of the Rockies. Upon waking, Doris was troubled by her dream. All day long she questioned how she could help. She kept exclaiming, "I'm an old lady. I can't work on the mountain, or the statue." After much soul-searching, the answer came to her. She could raise money for building the Lady. Again, her thoughts troubled her. How would she raise the money? One thing she always enjoyed doing was going to garage sales, so she mulled the idea of it in her mind. Somehow it seemed the thing to do, and now here was Doris, wanting to get permission to hold a garage sale for the Lady.

"I think it's a great idea, Doris, but you'll have to ask Joe Roberts for permission. I don't have the authority," I told her. "He should be at his office. But just tell him you want to put on a garage sale." After she left, I thought to myself, "I hope that's all she says. Joe isn't too keen about my talking to prayer groups, and I don't need his wrath so soon."

I saw her leaving Joe's office, and not two minutes after, Joe came across the yard doing the 440 yard dash with smoke coming out of his nostrils. I knew I was in for it now.

"See, I told you," he started yelling at me. "See what happens when you use the word, "miracles"? Now we have people coming down telling us they are seeing the Lady and talking to her."

"Joe," I interrupted his tirade, "the woman wants to help raise money for the statue. Let her!"

Joe continued with his anger against people and miracles. "Just recently a group came and prayed in front of the statue. One of them had cancer, and was asking to be cured. I went and invited them to use my office, so the newspaper wouldn't get wind of the story. We don't want a bunch of religious fanatics around here!" Joe continued on for a time, but my thoughts went back to the group he had mentioned.

I remembered the woman Joe was talking about. She had come to talk with me, and I was impressed with her sincerity. She was a pretty, young woman suffering from cancer, and her belief in the Blessed Mother was inspiring. She was hoping for a cure, but was also ready to die, if that's what the Lord willed. Before her death, about a week later, she requested all memorials be made to Our Lady of the Rockies. She must have known everyone in town, as the memorials poured in from all over the city.

Joe, finally running out of steam, left to go back to his office.

Mrs. Young was given permission to hold a garage sale. She returned to the prayer group and solicited their help. When she put an article in the paper asking people to donate to the garage sale, she was so overwhelmed with articles, she had to find a larger place. The amount of donations filled a school gymnasium. On the days of the sale, people came in droves to purchase the huge variety available to them. A total sum of twenty-five hundred dollars was proudly given to Our Lady by a little, elderly woman who at first thought there wasn't anything she could do to help. If it hadn't been for her dream, the money would never have been available to help buy poles and wire from the Montana Power. Half of the poles were donated, but the money from the garage sale made it possible to buy the other half. In fact, that garage sale was the catalyst for the yearly sale the Women's Auxiliary put on. Each year the donations pour in, and the amount now reaches between four and five thousand dollars. Doris Young will be remembered fondly by the Lady of the Rockies Foundation as the first person to instigate a garage sale for the Lady's benefit.

Not much had been accomplished on the statue for a while. Jack Warner kept me pretty busy with customer work. He never was exceptionally fond of the project, and every chance he got, he found something else for me to do. Roberts would rather I work on the statue, but for all practical purposes, the customer work is what keeps Roberts in business. When work comes rolling in, in order to keep busy, Ron Hughes pitches in and helps me. One job was rebuilding a one-hundred-fifty ton truck deck and cab which had been in an accident. For six weeks, Ron and I worked steadily on it, both of us anxious to be finished so we could return to the statue. When the truck was finally completed, we weren't positive just where we should commence again. In no time though, we were right back on target, ready to start on the left hand. We didn't figure the hand would take too long, as I had already constructed the right hand. The fingers were already assembled, so we felt this would be a breeze. We cut the sheets, attached the fingers to the base, and realized it wasn't as easy as it looked. We had become overconfident, and the Lady reminded us gently that it was she who was in control! After working diligently, we finally arranged the thumb to position correctly, then ground the welds down. We put plates on both the right and the left hands to bolt them to the arms of the statue. This being done, we turned the hands over to Randy Wixten to body fill and paint.

The hands leaning against the main shop at Roberts Equipment Co.

Joe Roberts entered the shop not long after the hands were completed. Surprisingly, he was very subdued, totally unlike him.
"What's wrong, Joe," I asked concerned over his appearance.
" I won't be around for awhile, LeRoy," Joe said haltingly. "I'm going into the hospital for an operation."
"How bad is it?" I asked him.
"They're not sure," Joe replied, "but while I'm gone, try to get as much done on the statue as you can. I'd really like to get the structure in front for Christmas."

"I've got both hands done, Joe, and as soon as I get done with the customer's equipment, we'll put the second section on the temporary four-foot legs, bring the skin down to the bottom of the legs, and set that section on the third permanent eight-foot inner section," I tried to reassure Joe, but felt that whatever the problem was, it was serious.

Several weeks passed, and Joe returned to the office. I was curious about what had transpired, but felt it was up to Joe to tell me. Somehow I sensed it was not good news, as Joe was reacting strangely. Then one day Roberts came into the shop to see how progress was going on the statue.

"I have cancer of the colon, LeRoy," Joe spoke softly. "But I have high hopes that everything will turn out O.K."

"I'll keep you in my prayers, Joe," I said struck dumbfounded by his announcement.

"Thanks, I appreciate it," Joe mumbled as he headed for the door and across the yard. I hadn't known what else to say, but was glad I had responded in that manner.

My faith had been greatly increased at this point due to my joining a Renew group offered by St. Anns Parish, and also to my many new friends from the prayer group sessions.

That evening, I telephoned Bob O'Bill and told him about Joe. He was as upset as I about the terrible news. We both agreed we'd pray to Mary and ask her to intercede for Joe.

Joe journeyed out of state for his operation. Prayer groups all over town were requested to implore God for restoration of Joe's health. People who didn't know Joe personally, but believed in what he was doing for the Lady, joined in prayer during his stay in the hospital.

On Joe's return to Butte, he immediately came to work to see how things were going.

"How are things going with you, Joe," I asked when he stopped at the shop.

"I'm really sore, LeRoy," Joe replied. "I hope no one ever has to go through what I did. The doctors think they've got it all, but couldn't make any promises."

"Everyone in Butte has sure been praying for you, Joe," I said. "Bob and I have offered special prayers to Our Lady for your recovery."

"You know, LeRoy," Joe went on. "You may not believe this, but I have always believed in the Blessed Mother. I pray to her all the time. I even have a statue of her in my house. Have I ever told you what she did for me?"

"No, you haven't Joe," I said surprised.

"Remember when we were down at Centennial Ave?" Joe asked me. I nodded my head yes.

"Do you also remember my partner, Les Sheridan, who was killed in the plane crash?" Joe went on.

"Yes, I remember about that. In fact, I was out looking for the plane on my snowmobile right after it happened," I replied.

"We all were," Joe remarked sadly. "Well, I not only lost a friend, but was left with a huge debt. I paid off most of it, but I still owed Wabco a large amount. Remember when they came and took over the business and operated it for awhile?"

"I sure do, it was pretty shaky for a time. I thought I was going to be looking for a new job," I said.

"Well you don't know how close we all came to looking for a new job. I was told if I didn't come up with the money by four o'clock that next Friday, that I would lose my business. I called everyone who owed me money, and told them if they didn't pay, I was going to lose my business. Everyone told me the same thing. They had run into hard times, too, and they didn't have the money to pay me. I went to the banks, but my credit was at its limit. I was heartsick. I went home to my room, where the statue is, and prayed to Mary. "Please," I implored her, "don't take away something I worked for all my life. Please, Mary, save my business."

"The next day, people who owed me money were coming in and paying me. In the mail came checks from more people. I was able to pay Wabco the money I owed them. Mary saved my business."

I thought to myself, "The Lord needed a place to have the statue of His mother built. That's why she saved Joe's business."

Joe was continuing with his story, "You should have seen the faces of the men from Wabco when I handed them their money. They couldn't believe it!"

When Joe left, I had to smile to myself, "And he doesn't believe in miracles! I just hope and pray that the Lady still needs Joe. She helped him then, would she help him now with his illness? What would happen to the statue if something happened to Joe? Would her Son want to see it finished? Oh, well, I'll let you take care of that, Mary. You've done all right so far."

CHAPTER TWENTY-THREE

CHRISTMAS 1984

I was always eager to retreat to the mountain site to work on the equipment, not only for the change of scene, but also to see the progress the "mountain men" had made. This time was no exception. As usual, they amazed me with the size and amount of rocks they had moved and how far they had advanced with the road in such rough terrain. Barth and Beavis tried to hurry me with the welding, as they were waiting to blast a section of rock. I quickly finished, and moved the welding truck from the blasting area. I crouched behind some rocks, hoping to see the blast, when Beavis came and advised me to find a rock to crawl under. I wondered why, but soon found out! When the blast went off, the rocks whistled by me. They were falling like hailstones. Afterwards, I joined Beavis standing on the site surveying the area.

"I wish I could spend more time up here," I said wistfully to Al. "It's so beautiful, like being in another world."

"Look," Beavis said, pointing at the panoramic view, "you can see seven mountain ranges from here."

"You know, Al," I remarked thoughtfully, "when I was a kid, I used to hike up here. I stood right here, but never did I think that there would be a statue here, especially one I built. Before my Dad passed away, he revealed how he loved this mountain. He requested to have his body cremated and his ashes spread over this area where we had hunted and hiked together. I didn't do it, Al. I buried him in the cemetery instead. Now that the statue is going here, I feel remorse in not honoring his request. "

Bob O'Bill and Al Beavis were hoping to get the base on the mountain before the snow came, but it didn't look as though they would make it until the next spring. Bob would be out of town for the winter. The Montana Power was sending him to Bozeman on a big job. Without Bob to ramrod the project, it will probably grind to a standstill. That's what happened two years ago when we were building the inner structure. If Bob didn't come at night, no one else would either. I never saw any two men that could get people to work for them like Bob O'Bill and Bill Barth. They are just impossible to say no to.

Meanwhile, back at Roberts yard, we are getting ready to put the fourth section together, the one the hands will be attached to. The folds draping over her arms proved to be rather difficult. All the time my thoughts kept going to how she would look when completed. Each piece that went together increased my eagerness to see the whole structure on the mountain.

So far, this year had been a cold one, and Christmas was once again on the horizon. Joe wanted the four sections in front for the Holiday Season, so we really had to hustle. Even though the temperature was fluctuating between twenty and thirty below zero, we were forced to work outside on the statue because of its size. My face was sore due to the extreme cold, but Ron was faring much better because of his beard. We worked as long as we could stand the freezing cold, then we moved to the inside to get warm. I developed a cold and my chest was aching, but I was too stubborn to stay home and take care of it. I kept telling Pat that if I croaked, I wanted my ashes to be placed up with the statue.

As I was coughing and wheezing away, I noticed a young lady in her late twenties watching the progress. Her name was Jeri Bertoglio and she was enthralled with the beauty of the statue. Her little girl was just as impressed and always wanted to put money in the donation box whenever they visited. Being young and just getting started in life, Jeri had little to spare, but still wanted to help in some way. Jeri had made an afghan called "Log Cabin Quilt" which had taken eighty hours of labor. Jeri had displayed the afghan in a booth at the annual Hawthorne Bazaar. Raffle tickets had been sold on the quilt. It was exquisite! Two hundred fifty dollars had been donated to the Lady from the raffle.

Bob O'Bill had come in on a weekend to see how everything was progressing. I related the story of the afghan to him. He just smiled and mentioned what had happened last summer to him. An older couple had arrived in Butte and happened to see the uncompleted statue in front of Roberts. It was a Saturday, and the shop was closed, but the couple spent some time looking through the fence at the statue. George James, the watchman, came out to visit with them. He referred them to Bob O'Bill when they asked to talk to someone about the statue. They drove an old truck one hundred sixty miles from Great Falls, Montana. The man handed Bob twelve, one hundred dollar bills and said, "God bless you people".

Bob was stunned. The couple looked as though they needed the money more than the Lady. The man explained why he made the donation. During their lifetime, they had the privilege of having twelve beautiful children. They all grew up to be good, responsible adults, faithful to their religion, and held excellent jobs. He and his wife had prayed to Mary every day for their children, and now they wanted to help Mary get on the mountain. Bob tried to take their names for the records, and to send them thank you cards from the Lady, but the man would have no part of it. He trusted Bob to give it to the fund, and did not feel the need of a thank you. His thank you was in the form of twelve beautiful children. Bob gave the money to Roberts, and the year after, the couple returned with another donation of twelve hundred dollars.

"Don't stories like these make it all worth it, Bob?" I remarked. "People pour out what they have in money, material, labor, or just their love."

"The Lady has plans for Butte, LeRoy. It's great to be part of it, isn't it?" answered Bob.

Around this time, Lynn Keeley was hired by Joe Roberts to assist John Kelly in handling the memorials. The job had become overwhelming along with his other duties. Bob O'Bill and some of the other workers were unhappy with the hiring, as they felt a volunteer could be found to do the work. When he confronted Joe, Joe exerted his authority as President and overruled Bob. I tried to pacify Bob by telling him I thought Lynn was doing a good job. She acted as a guide in explaining the statue, which relieved me of doing it. That left more time to work on the statue. I had heard she was also delving into obtaining grant money.

As Christmas neared, Joe was getting impatient to move the completed sections to the front again. On Friday before Christmas, Ron and I were about ready, but Dave Barker, the crane operator, was sent out of town. Joe promised Dave would be back by ten o'clock, so Ron and I proceeded to get everything in order for the move. Before we were too far into the preparations, Jack Warner came in with a rush order from one of the mines. A bucket from a loader needed work, and couldn't wait until after Christmas. I tried arguing with Warner, but without success. I kept insisting Joe wanted the statue in front that afternoon, and Jack kept insisting the bucket needed to be done. Being a supervisor, he won, but not without a fight for the Lady. Warner was concerned about keeping the doors of the place open, while I wanted to get the Lady out in front for Joe. Being in a dilemma about what to do first, I beckoned for

Ron to come over and help me with the bucket for the loader. I figured if we could double up, we could accomplish the job twice as fast, then we could work on the Lady. We worked right through lunch, and were hurrying as fast as we could when Roberts came storming up to the shop. He was adamant about putting the statue in front right away. Luckily, we were just about done with the bucket. Around one o'clock, we were back working on the Lady. We worked furiously until around four-thirty, positioning the hand section, then bringing up the bust section to sit it on. Everyone else in the shop had quit for the day, and were in the office having their annual Christmas party, except for the four of us: Dave Barker, Jim Dunn, Ron, and myself. When I walked up the boom of the crane and got on the hook, they all came to the window to watch. Somehow word got out, and while the procedure was going on, people were driving up, taking pictures and watching us. Cars and trucks on the highway directly above us, were stopping to see what transpiring. Lynn decided to call the radio and TV stations for news coverage. Dave lifted me up to the head and I placed the hook into the eye; then he set the head on the bust section. I waited until Dunn and Ron bolted the legs, then Dave lowered me on the hook. The four of us went inside the statue, and bolted the rings of the sections together. Finally, we fastened the hands to the section. When we were done, we went to have a look at her. I was stunned by the amount of people that had stopped to view her. But I could see why when I gazed up at the most beautiful sight in the world. She was exquisite!

Someone yelled, "How tall is it?"

In answer, I replied, "Fifty-four feet!" The crowd murmured and I heard a large "WOW" from one of them. Someone asked me if I would give a statement on a radio program. Recalling how angry Joe had gotten last time, I had the good sense to refer them to Roberts.

As we were standing there admiring the statue, I noticed that all the employees of Roberts were standing out in sub-zero weather watching us, not even noticing the cold. They were as proud as we were. After a while, we went inside to warm the outside of our bodies. The inside still remained warm from the feeling we had received from the whole experience of putting this much together. I noticed Joe over to the side and went over to talk to him.

"What a wonderful gift for all the people of Butte who have donated to the Lady," I remarked. "We put the Mother of Jesus Christ out in front for Christmas!"

Grinning from ear-to-ear, Joe replied, "I already talked to Bob O'Bill. He and other electricians will be down to put lights on her tonight, so it will be lit for Christmas Eve."

I went home and watched the whole thing on TV, feeling so proud. Later, I took Pat and the family down to look at her. We weren't the only ones looking. There was a string of cars driving by. All the other years, people would drive around town looking at Christmas lights. This year of 1984, they were out to see Our Lady. Pat was astounded at the size and beauty of the statue.

"How do you plan on getting her to the top of the mountain when she is completed?" Pat asked wondrously.

"I don't know," I answered. "I'm not going to worry about it. The Lady got us this far. Let her worry about that part."

On the way past the Lady, we decided to stop and see how Bob O'Bill was doing, as he only lived a few blocks away. He was flying as high as I was. He felt badly that he was working out of town, and could only be back on the weekends. He hoped the job would not last beyond spring, so he could get back to the Lady.

The next day, I couldn't stay away from the Lady. I had to go see her again. Everyone but George James was gone. He remarked how crazy it had been ever since the Lady had gone up. The steady stream of cars had increased instead of decreased, and every car stopped and put in a donation. Things were looking good for the Lady.

As I stood there, thoughts of my Renew group came to me. They had given so much support during this time, I wanted to show my appreciation in some way. I hurried to the welding shop and took some of the scrap iron from the statue. I drew and cut out a cross, then I welded brass on the front of it. It looked like a gold cross, ten inches in height and six inches across. I drilled a hole in the center, and put my initials on the back of it. Happy with my decision, I felt I had the perfect gift for everyone. I made enough of them for everyone in the group. They all felt they had a piece of the statue, which indeed, they did. I made an extra one for Roberts, as I felt it was appropriate that he should have one, too. He was as delighted as the rest of the people. I also suggested we sell them as a money-maker. Joe thought the idea was a good one, and we still sell them. Pat wanted one, and she made sure that she got the best one. I can't tell the difference!

CHAPTER TWENTY-FOUR

OUR LADY WRITES A SONG

A few weeks before Christmas, Mark Staples gave a concert to raise money for The Lady. Mark received a standing ovation for singing his song, "Our Lady of the Rockies." After the concert, Pat and I had an opportunity to relate to Mark how much we enjoyed his singing, especially the song, "Our Lady of the Rockies." I shared some of the stories from the building of the statue, and Mark shared how he came to write the song.

Mark had heard about the statue from his family still residing in Butte. He had telephoned Joe Roberts offering to do a concert as a fund raiser for Our Lady. Joe was excited that Mark had offered his talents, especially his willingness to write a song. Mark had just won a contest entitling him to one thousand dollars, as well as a first-class, all-expense-paid trip to Nashville, Tennessee, to compete in a national contest. Mark was accustomed to riding coach style, and the difference between first class and coach was seven hundred dollars. Feeling that the money could be put to better use, he cashed in the first class ticket for a coach ticket. Adding the difference to his thousand dollars, he was able to schedule a recording session in Los Angeles immediately following his trip to Nashville. He had the idea of doing a song called, "A Mining City Christmas" and "Our Lady of the Rockies" as a specialty tape which could be sold at the December benefit. It would also be used to promote the upcoming event. The words for "Mining City Christmas" had already been written, but "Our Lady of the Rockies" was drawing a complete blank.

Mark had been more successful than he planned in Nashville. His time was limited to one day recording in Los Angeles instead of the four he had planned on.

Arriving in Los Angeles, Mark immediately reported to the studio, putting down the music tracks without voice or words to a "Mining City Christmas" and another song. These songs took about two or three of the five hours allotted for the instrumental portion. When it came time to play "Our Lady of the Rockies," he still had no melody, much less the lyrics. He asked the technicians to give him a few minutes to doodle; whatever he came up with would be the melody and then while the music tracks were being mastered, he could write the lyrics.

He tried to get the feel of a little country church in the melody, but was really struggling with it. Given the time deadline, he remembered sitting back on his piano stool in the little room he was in and saying to himself, "What is it I'm trying to accomplish here?" He realized what he wanted to write was a prayer. It occurred to him that the best way to write a prayer was by saying a prayer. At this time, he began to absentmindedly play the piano while he was thinking of what it was that he hoped the Our Lady of the Rockies project would bring to Butte. The basic melody materialized and he was about to try to create some clever expansion of it, when it also occurred to him that the heart and soul of this hymn should be simplicity. He made the decision to basically have "Our Lady of the Rockies" repeat itself similarly throughout, but with different levels of intensity and arrangement.

Moments later he recorded the music, and as the technicians went about mixing and mastering the music on the three songs, he set about in the next hour or so to write the lyrics for the hymn. Again, he became bogged down for most of that time, and again, it was because he was trying to create the song rather than let the song come through him. With about ten minutes to go before he was supposed to sing "Our Lady of the Rockies," and only two hours before his plane was leaving for Montana, he again sat back at the desk and said, "Wait a minute! What am I doing here?"

He forced himself back to zero in on what the whole idea was. He was supposed to write a hymn representing the hopes and aspirations of a community as they were reflected in a massive project that could hopefully renew their sense of community. He admitted he could never focus on the idea of the statue as a celebration of motherhood. To Mark, it represented the heart of Butte, an indomitable belief in community, and an unwillingness to accept any limits of what could be envisioned and accomplished together.

Once again, Mark turned his thoughts from lyric writing and just simply said a prayer asking for those blessings for which he himself felt so desperately in need, both for his family and the community.

Mark is reluctant to attribute the breakthroughs in his life to miracles, not because he is timid to acknowledge the presence of divine grace, but rather because he feels that life itself is a miracle and is in itself the greatest manifestation of heaven's gifts to us. Still, he does feel it rather miraculous that the prayer he wrote at that moment, and the blessings he asked for, fit the music that had been written moments before as if they had been together through the ages.

The best was yet to come. As he began to run through his vocals for the recording of the hymn, he heard a choir practicing in the sound studio next door. His understanding was that they were a professional Los Angeles Choir. Filled with the sense that Our Lady of the Rockies was a dream of monumental impact for anyone that became involved in it, Mark went next door and boldly asked them to accompany him in the song. They listened to Mark's story about the community and Our Lady, and agreed (to his surprise) to sing with him.

Mark almost missed his plane that evening, but he made sure the demo tape was in his pocket . He presented the tape to Joe Roberts, but he was dismayed when he saw a drawing of the Lady with her hands folded in prayer. As he had already recorded the words "may our hearts be like your arms, full of love and open wide," he thought he would have to do the song over. When he said this to Roberts, Joe laughed and showed him the new drawing of the Lady, whose arms had been unfolded and open to all.

He still had not heard the song on the demo tape, and later when he was driving his car, he heard the song on the radio. He became so overcome with emotion on hearing the beautiful song that he had to pull over to the side of the road. He knew then the song had come from Our Lady. Many groups and individuals have chosen this hymn for their weddings, funerals, and religious holidays.

OUR LADY OF THE ROCKIES

Bless us, Our Lady of the Rockies,
And this land those peaks divide;
May our hearts be like your arms,
Full of love and open wide.

Give us strength in times of trouble,
Give us faith in times of fear;
When the dark is all around us,
Light our way and hold us near.

Bless us, Our Lady of the Rockies,
And this land those peaks divide;
May our hearts be like your arms,
Full of love and open wide.

Like a river ever flowing,
Each of us is born to share;
The joy in living is in giving,
Teach us how and hear our prayer.

Our Lady, rise above for all eyes to see,
The peace and hope that you bring;
Make us all one family,
Give us one voice to sing.

Bless us, Our Lady of the Rockies,
And this land those peaks divide;
May our hearts be like your arms,
Full of love and open wide.

by   Mark Staples

CHAPTER TWENTY-FIVE

"IT'S NOT BROKEN!"

The completed sections of the statue remained in front of Roberts for about a week after the holidays. Finally, we disassembled the bottom section in preparation for the fifth piece which would be under it. The head and shoulders sections remained in front of Roberts for people to view when they drove by. Many favorable comments had been received by those who had seen the statue in front.

As the months went by, Ron Hughes and I continued to work on the next section, even though the temperature fluctuated between thirty-five and forty below zero that winter. We would work inside as much as possible, but when it came time to weld pieces onto the large structure, we would have to dress warm and brave the elements.

I had just taken a piece out to weld onto the structure, climbed the ladder, and put my helmet on to start welding. All of a sudden, I was laying across the ladder on the ground. Everything had happened so fast, I was dazed. As I lay there, I could see what had occurred. The back legs of the ladder collapsed causing a sudden drop of about eight feet. I landed on my leg which had gotten tangled in the ladder. I remained there for some time, unable to move. Ron was welding on the other side of the structure and didn't hear me shouting for him. When he did come around on his way back to the shop to get warm, he noticed me struggling to free myself. I was in a great deal of pain, but managed, with Ron's help, to return to the welding shop. The warmth of the shop comforted me, and I began to feel a little better. My right leg was swollen, and my back throbbed with pain. Ron offered to drive me to the doctor, but I refused, preferring to do it on my own. Leaving him with instructions to tell Warner what had happened and where I was going, I gingerly got behind the wheel of my truck. As I was leaving Roberts' shop, I faced another dilemma. Should I go see a chiropractor for my back or should I go see an orthopedic doctor for my leg? A week or so ago, I had injured my back getting down from the Hyster, and since my back was hurting now, I decided to see Dr. Paulman, the chiropractor.

After describing what had happened, I showed Dr. Paulman my leg. When he saw how swollen it was, he refused to touch my back until I had some x-rays taken of my leg. The results of the x-rays revealed my bone had a hairline fracture by the hip. He lent me some crutches, and told me to go home and keep the weight off my leg. At one o'clock, I was to report back to him, pick up my x-rays, and be at Dr. Murphy's office by 1:30. He had called the orthopedic doctor and arranged for an appointment that afternoon.

At one o'clock, I returned to the chiropractor's office. He took me in to explain the x-rays. There was a line running at a forty-five degree angle across my bone. Again he stressed the importance of not walking on my leg. He said any pressure on the leg might cause the line to fracture.

On the way to Dr. Murphy's office, I passed Roberts' yard and looked over at Mary's face.

"Mary," I said, "If you want me to finish you, I won't be able to do it with a broken leg." I arrived at Dr. Murphy's office at exactly one-thirty. He examined me, then referred to the x-rays I had brought with me.

"I'm not sure whether it's broken or not," Dr. Murphy said.

"But, Dr. Paulman showed me the line across the bone," I replied.

"LeRoy, your leg is so swollen, I can't be sure. It could be cracked, or it could be a blood muscle line. What I want you to do is go home, stay off the leg, and keep ice on it until the swelling goes down. I don't want you to go to the bathroom without those crutches. I'll see you in a couple of days," Dr. Murphy stated emphatically.

My son was playing a basketball game that evening, and by then I was tired of sitting in the chair with nothing to do but watch television. So, I gathered myself, crutches and all, and accompanied my wife to the game. Being on crutches didn't slow me down at all. They just made walking more of a challenge, and I love a challenge. The next night, the basketball game was being held in Dillon, Montana, so Pat and I decided to attend it.

During the day, I was so bored, that no matter how much pain I was experiencing, I was bound and determined to do something even if I had to use crutches to do it. I found all sorts of things of ways to make the crutches useful. I used them as an extension of my arms to drag things to me when I couldn't reach them. The morning after the game in Dillon, I came out of the bedroom without my crutches. Pat reminded me what the doctor had said about putting weight on my leg.

"It's not broken," I replied. "I told Mary if it was broken, I couldn't work on her. I don't feel that my leg is broken, and I don't need these stupid crutches any more. I want to get back to work."

A few days later, I walked into Dr. Murphy's office. He looked at me and wanted to know how long I had been walking without the crutches. When I said five days, he wanted to know whether it still hurt or not. After shaking my head no, he insisted I take one more week from work, at least.

"No!" I said determined to have my way. "I have to get back to work on the statue if we are ever going to get it on the mountain."

Seeing the stubborn look on my face, Dr. Murphy gave in with a sigh. "Alright," he said. "but if it hurts, I want you to get right back to me."

Ron had finished what he could on the welding, and was trying to look busy when I showed up the next day.

"Everyone said your leg was broken and you wouldn't be back for months," Ron said, happy to see me. He had been worried Roberts was going to advise him to stay home until I returned. He had just discovered the girl he was going with was pregnant with his child, and he didn't need to lose the two hundred dollars a week he was making. In fact, he had been talking about looking for another job, as he really needed the money, especially now.

"You don't think the Lady would let that happen, now, do you?" I replied, smiling.

Not long after that, I was asked to give a talk at the "Here We Are Lord" prayer group which meets at St. Anns Parish. As I was sitting there watching the people come in, I almost fell from the chair. Dr. Paulman, the chiropractor had just come in the door. I walked over to him.

"What are you doing here?" I asked. "Did you know I was talking tonight?"

"No, are you?" Dr. Paulman answered.

"Yeah, but what made you come here? Do you belong to this prayer group?" I wanted to know.

"One of my patients mentioned it to me. She thought I might enjoy it. Then later one of the women working in the next office came in for coffee and mentioned it also. So, I thought, why not try it?" Dr. Paulman replied.

"I'm going to talk about falling and injuring my leg," I continued. "If I ask, would you say something?"

"Sure," he agreed.

As I sat there, I still couldn't believe this man came to a prayer group just because someone said he might enjoy it.

I gave my talk and when it was time, I related how I hurt my leg and what happened afterwards. I called on Dr. Paulman to verify what I had just said. Unhesitating, he came to the front of the room.

"I have been a doctor for ten years," he started. "It took me four years to become a chiropractor learning the same material as a medical doctor. We don't attend college for the same length of time as a medical doctor, as we don't have need for all the knowledge they must learn. I have taken thousands of x-rays, and in my opinion, LeRoy's leg was a fracture. I just wish I had a picture of the x-ray to show you, but the x-ray needs special lighting. For the life of me, I don't know why I came here tonight, but I'm glad I did. I feel, I had witnessed a miracle."

I just sat there and thanked Mary.

CHAPTER TWENTY-SIX

THE POWER OF PRAYER

Joe Roberts informed me I wasn't to talk to any more prayer groups. He and Bob O'Bill had been requested by the Bishop of the Helena Diocese not to be relating the miracles concerning the Lady, as cults could be attracted and problems could arise. The bishop would have to verify all the happenings as true before he could give his approval to them. He was taking a "wait and see" attitude, although he did not entirely dismiss the idea of future happenings. I felt Joe was just telling me that because the statue had been declared nondenominational and for mothers everywhere. Even though most religions recognize the Mother of God, great care would have to be taken to include all religions in Our Lady of the Rockies statue. Bob mentioned the same information. I was dumbfounded!

"Bob," I exclaimed, "if we don't tell people what the Lord has done in our lives, how will they know what happened building the statue of His Mother?"

"LeRoy, my mind is made up. The bishop asked us not to discuss the stories, and I'm going along with him," Bob walked away from me and out the door. I was stunned. What had happened in Helena with the bishop? Why didn't the bishop want these stories told? I had been scheduled to talk to the bishop with Joe and Bob, but Joe didn't inform me until after the talk was concluded. Joe insisted I was too busy. If I had been there, maybe I would have been able to understand the reasons more clearly hearing it directly from the bishop. I felt very dejected over what had transpired.

When I went home that evening, I discussed the matter with Pat, hoping to make some sense out of the whole thing. Pat felt maybe this was a sign I wasn't supposed to talk any more.

"Maybe it's time for someone else to pick up the cross and tell the stories, LeRoy. Maybe Mary just wants you to build her, and let someone else do the verbalizing," Pat suggested.

"Pat, I don't enjoy getting up in front of people and talking. I wish with all my heart someone else would. But have you seen anyone else doing it? When I went to the Daughters of Isabella dinner with Bob, I felt the Lady was telling me she wanted me to share with others what she had done. I don't know what to make of it any more," I said.

As the days passed, I kept thinking what Pat had said. Maybe I should discontinue speaking. I took her advice to pray on it, and let Mary take charge. That night, my son Rob, had a basketball game at the Civic Center. There were two games scheduled, with Deer Lodge, Montana, playing the first one against Butte Central. As we were sitting there waiting for the second game to start, (the one Rob was to play in), a lady approached me. Sitting on the other side of the Civic Center, she had spotted me in the crowd. After the game, she had planned on telephoning me to invite me to speak at the Deer Lodge prayer group the next month. She was delighted to have seen me, saving herself a telephone call. Not knowing how to get out of it gracefully, I decided to tell her the truth. The bishop had requested me not to give any more talks. I could see the disappointment on her face, as I had never refused anyone before. I visited with her for awhile. Then as the second game was about to start, she stood up to leave. As she advanced down the row of seats, she stopped and came back.

"Pray about it," she said, "you have touched so many people's hearts. That's all we hear about in Deer Lodge. Think about it, and give me a call, please." She handed me a card with her name and telephone number on it, then left quickly.

For a couple of days, I thought about it off and on. After many prayers to Our Lady, I decided not to go. I felt this was the thing to do as long as Joe and Bob were so adamant about not talking. I didn't need the hassle any more. I gave the woman a call that evening. She was disappointed, but said she understood. Three weeks later, out of the blue, Pat and I decided to attend the prayer group meeting being held at St. Johns. We seldom went to this meeting, as we were attending the one at St. Anns instead. Both of us felt the need for prayers that night since we had missed Monday night's prayer group.

Peggy Racicot, the speaker, spoke about evangelizing. She stressed the point that if people didn't share what God has done in their lives, how would other people know how compassionate He is? Sitting there listening to her, a feeling of remorse came over me. I wondered if this was what I came to hear. Did Mary send me here for a reason? Did I let her down by not speaking at the Deer Lodge prayer group? My thoughts were still mixed up. After the talk, I went over to the table to have some coffee and cookies. Six ladies from Deer Lodge had come over to the prayer group that evening. They approached me and asked if I was coming to Deer Lodge to speak the next evening. I was shocked. I had told the lady on the phone my decision not to come, and here these women were, asking me if I was ready to speak tomorrow night!

"I told the lady three weeks ago I wasn't coming. Didn't she get another speaker?" I asked surprised.

"No," the lady replied, "we have all been praying that you'd come. We had hoped you would be here tonight." I just sat there with my mouth opened. I couldn't believe they had waited and prayed this long for me to speak to them at their prayer group. What could I say, but yes! I made them promise not to say a word to anyone about my coming to talk. I didn't want word to get back to Roberts or Bob.

The next morning about ten o'clock, Joe came into the welding shop.

"When you go to Deer Lodge tonight, take some crosses with you," Joe took delight in dropping his little bomb.

"How did you know?" I asked.

"A lady came into our gift shop and asked if you would bring a bunch of crosses to their meeting tonight," Joe said. "Don't tell any of your stories! Remember what the bishop said. Why don't you write down what you plan on saying, and I'll look it over?"

I didn't say anything, but I thought to myself, "Whatever I say will come from the Lord, not from Joe."

That evening when I spoke, the audience loved it. I told all the stories, even though I knew Joe and Bob would be angry with me. After these ladies had gone through three weeks of prayer, I felt they had the right to hear my usual talk, miracles and all. One woman made a very good point. She felt I talked about Mary excessively, instead of being more Christ-centered. Mary should lead all people to Christ. She was right, I had been too Mary-centered, and not Christ-centered enough.

The lady who had ordered the cross came forward and asked about them. I felt like giving her a lecture, but smiled instead She hadn't realized the position she had put me in, and it had all worked out any way. When I brought her cross from the car into the building, more people approached to buy a cross, too. Twenty-five of them were sold, even the priest bought one. The next day, I presented Joe with three hundred seventy-five dollars from the crosses. When he asked if I had told any stories, I just smiled and walked away.

Marilyn Boyle from our Renew Group mentioned a Cursillo that was coming up soon. Not knowing what it was, she explained it as a short course on Christianity. For three days, a concentration on Christ was presented, then afterwards, follow-up sessions would keep that love for Christ renewed. I looked at Marilyn suspiciously.

"Marilyn, I can't keep my mind on Mass for an hour. How can I go and do it for three days?" I laughed at her suggestion.

A few days later, Tubie Johnson, a good friend, asked me to do the same thing. I glanced at him the same way, and told him no thanks, too. He was planning on working this Cursillo, and suggested I ask Mary for further direction. He knew that would get me there, but I wasn't so sure. I'm not one to sit still for any length of time, let alone listen to speeches all day long. I just laughed at him and let it go.

The next morning, I parked in my usual place in front of the head and shoulders of the Lady. As I walked past the head, I thought of what Tubie had asked of me. So I looked up into her face and said jokingly, "You want me to go to a Cursillo?" I laughed and walked on thinking how I could tell Tubie that I asked the Lady about the Cursillo.

That night at the dinner table, all of a sudden, I jumped up and called Marilyn on the phone. I heard myself telling her I would make the Cursillo. No one was more surprised than I was. I was very reluctant to go and sit for three days, but sure enough, the next weekend found me on my way to Dillon, where the Cursillo was to take place.

There were sixty men at the Cursillo. We ate, sang, prayed and hugged each other for three days. It was one of the more beautiful experiences of my life. It was there I really came to know Jesus, Mary's Son. My faith journey made a giant leap forward that weekend. During the Cursillo, we belonged to a small group or family. The men in the group were to share some of their life experiences with each other. I, naturally, was so full of the Lady, I shared for some time. When we were finished and getting ready to leave, one of the men asked me what the statue needed that they could pray for. I told them they were trying to find a helicopter that would be able to lift a great deal of weight. Their prayers would be very welcome.

Monday came, and I returned to work. I was still flying high from my encounter with Christ. I received a phone call around nine o'clock in the office. When I answered it a man said, "I'm Joe Monahan. I'm calling from Washington, D.C."

I worked with Ed Monahan, his brother, the tool man at Robert's. When Ed had talked to his mother, Rose, about the statue, he mentioned we needed a helicopter to lift the Lady to the mountain when the time came. Joe Monahan worked for the Senate Library in Washington, and his mother discussed with him how we were looking for a helicopter to transport the statue. Joe had promised to look into things and see what he could come up with in Washington. Now here he was on the phone telling me he was trying to get a helicopter for the Lady. I couldn't believe it! Talk about the power of prayer!

"A helicopter would cost about fifteen hundred dollars per hour for the lift," Monahan continued. "I'm going to to try to get a grant to pay for it, though."

I thanked him for his offer, stunned that I had been summoned to the phone when Joe Roberts, a friend of his, should have been talking to him instead. Then it dawned on me what had happened. I would not have known about the telephone call if Roberts had received it. This was the Lady's way of telling me the prayers of those men at the Cursillo were very strong and powerful.

CHAPTER TWENTY-SEVEN

MARY FINDS THE KEYS

The spring weather cooperated allowing us to accomplish the completion of another section of the statue. Again, Joe Roberts wanted the statue in front for Mother's Day. Even though another section was completed, I did not feel it wise to assemble all the sections together without a strong base to support it. Dave Barker agreed with me and discussed the project with Joe. Joe finally conceded to leave things remain as they were. Every time we put the sections together, so much time was spent bolting and unbolting the sections, the completion of the statue was delayed. Another consideration was the wind. If a gusty wind developed, it could possibly topple the statue, destroying what had taken us years to establish. It just wasn't worth the chance.

Bob O'Bill reported he had located a facility where we could acquire the use of a helicopter. The company required sixty-thousand dollars just to bring it to Butte, and six thousand dollars, per hour to use it. On top of that, the helicopter would only elevate twelve thousand pounds, which meant we would have to cut and ring each section again. It would require another year if we were to execute that. Shaking my head, I hoped this would not transpire. When Roberts heard the proposal, he suggested we haul the sections with a truck. This sounded even more ridiculous and I hoped he was just kidding. Mary had better get busy and make her plans known and she did.

Roberts had received a call from Joe Monahan in Washington, D.C. Monahan had talked John Melcher, a Senator from Montana, Stan Kimmet, and Barry Goldwater from Arizona, to try to get approval from the government for the use of a helicopter. Monahan was really doing a splendid job in Washington. We kept him in our prayers all the time. He was quite the persuader for Mary.

In the meantime, we were not without minor troubles on the road to the mountain. One day on my way to do some welding, I was unable to unlock the gate. On further examination, I found a piece of wood wedged in the hole where the key was supposed to fit. Evidently, someone had gotten angry when they were incapable of unlocking the gate and decided to make sure no one else got in, either. The next week, someone pushed a big rock into the gate, bending it quite severely. I spent a long time repairing what the vandals had thought was a great idea. Every time we went up to the site, we were expecting something to be wrong. Many people, especially kids, don't like to be reminded to stay out. It is a challenge to prove otherwise.

Mike Cerise had come down to obtain a loader and a compressor to start drilling the holes for the rods to go in. This would be the start of the base.

"I sure wish O'Bill was here," Mike stated. "With Bob in Flathead, it's really hard to get equipment. Barth takes care of getting men for the job, but Bob is the go-getter for the equipment. Barth wants to start the base, but I'm having a hard time getting the right equipment."

"Don't let it worry you, Mike," I tried to reassure him. "Billy Fisher is having the same trouble. Bob told him to level off the site as soon as the snow is gone, but because it is too rocky he is unable to do it. Nothing seems to go right unless Bob is here, does it?"

A few weeks later, Roberts came down to the welding shop. Father Kevin O'Neill, Father Byrnes, and Father Harris were in his office requesting to go to the mountain. Joe wanted me to take them, as he knew how much I enjoyed visiting the site.

As we labored up the switchbacks, the vehicle rebelled and just quit. I felt terrible having everyone walk the rest of the way to the site. The priests reassured me they didn't mind; in fact, they welcomed the chance to stretch their legs. The four of us recited the Rosary as we trudged up the steep hillside. When we reached the top, Earl Casagranda was putting in dirt and leveling it off. I instructed the priests to investigate the area where the statue would be while I returned to the vehicle to try once more to start it.

On my return to the site, the priests were still engaged in marveling over the wonderful site and panoramic view from the mountain. I picked up rocks, throwing them over the side, while I waited for the priests to go back down. The priests had used up all the time they had, so we proceeded to descend the mountain. When we encountered the main gate, I realized with great dismay that I no longer had the keys. Somewhere between here and the top of the mountain, they had become lost. Reluctantly, I informed the priests of my plight, and gave them the choice of remaining with the vehicle, or returning with me to the site. They opted to remain at the gate, as it was a beautiful day, and they were enjoying the scenery.

As I advanced up the road once more, I felt the need for some prayers, as I had absolutely no idea where I might have dropped the keys. I asked Our Lady to help in the process of looking for the keys so the priests would not have a long wait. I arrived at the top gate and searched the area thoroughly, but to no avail. My next decision was to return to the top of the mountain where Earl was still spreading dirt over the site.

When I related what had happened to Earl, he asked if I remembered where I had been standing. I pointed to an area, and Earl just shook his head saying I was out of luck. They had just dumped two fresh loads of dirt on that spot, and he had already raked over the pile. Panicking, I picked up the rake and trotted over to where I had been standing earlier.

Earl hurried over to stop me and said, "What are you doing? There is six inches of dirt there. Those keys could be anywhere! You'll have to dig up the whole area. You'll never find them in a million years! It's like looking for a needle in a haystack!"

Earl was probably right, but I had to try anyway. I clenched the rake in my hands, and burrowed down into the pile of dirt. Bringing the tines of the rake to the top of the pile, I noticed a shiny object hanging perilously from one of the teeth. We looked at it in disbelief. There on the ends of the rake were the keys I had prayed I would find!

"I can't believe it!" cried Earl excitedly. "You could have lost them anywhere and after the first try, you drag them up!"

As I walked back to the truck, I remembered to thank Mary. She alone was responsible for my finding the keys. When I arrived back at the gate where I had left the priests, I remarked, "You must have said a lot of prayers."

"We did!" they refrained. When I told them of the incident, they weren't even surprised. One of them smiled and quipped, "It was the power of prayer."

The Pre-Release Center requested to send a couple of men to volunteer their labor on the statue. This is a center where men about to be released from prison can become adjusted to regular living conditions gradually. The two men arrived and began to grind on the welds. One of them expressed an interest in the shirts with Our Lady on them. Noting his interest, I asked Roberts if he could spare a couple of shirts for the pre-release workers. Joe was happy to, as they were receiving no pay. The one who asked about the shirt wore his regularly, while the other one took it to the Center. When he tried to give it to the receptionist, she informed him it was the picture of the Blessed Mother. On hearing this, he smiled and reclaimed it so he could send it to his mother. He wanted her to know he was working on a statue of the Blessed Mother. The men frequently went into the office where the gift shop was located. One of them expressed a desire to purchase some of the cards with Our Lady on them. Lynn told him the price, and he frowned, as he did not possess a dollar to buy one. Lynn, feeling sorry for him, gave him a dollar. He, in turn, gave the dollar back to her for the cards. Smiling, he reported that he was going to send the cards home to his mother to show her what he was doing. Lynn felt quite pleased about that. The Lady has touched many people in many different ways.

CHAPTER TWENTY-EIGHT

MARY ANSWERS A MOTHER'S PRAYER

On Father's Day, Ron Hughes and his girlfriend camped at Georgetown Lake west of Anaconda, Montana. Although her baby wasn't due for two months, labor started prematurely that weekend. Ron rushed her to Anaconda. As they pulled up to her mother's house, her water broke. Knowing that the birth was imminent, Ron sped on to the hospital in Butte. Ron became a father that day. When Ron came into work Monday, he spoke of his experiences of becoming a father. Noticing the worry in his eyes, I was aware of something being drastically wrong.

"LeRoy," Ron began, "after the baby was born, Mary and I were elated. When we discussed the baby's future, we decided to bring it up Catholic."

This surprised me, as Ron had never talked about religion. In fact, he had even told me once he thought he was an atheist. All the times I would talk about the stories connected with the Lady, Ron had remained silent.

Ron continued with his story. "We were expressing our happiness in having the labor and stress over with when the doctor entered the room. We both sensed that something was wrong. The doctor compassionately explained to us the baby wasn't expected to live. Because of its prematurity, the lungs were underdeveloped and the baby was experiencing respiratory problems. The liver was also not functioning correctly and yellow jaundice was evident. When the doctor left, we just stared at each other, both recalling instances in our first marriages concerning a child. Tears welled up in Mary's eyes, and she moaned, "Not again." I knew what she was talking about. In her first marriage, she had anguished over the loss of her first child shortly after birth. I had also had a similar experience in my first marriage. My first baby, a son, had died soon after he was born. It seemed our hearts were to be broken yet another time."

"Mary struggled to get out of bed. Startled, I asked her what she was doing. Mary lowered herself to her knees along side the bed. She haltingly said she hasn't been faithful in attending church, but she had been raised Catholic, and her parents still practiced their faith. She was going to ask Our Lady for the life of her child. As she knelt there by the side of the bed, tears streaming down her face, I heard her tell the Blessed Mother how she had been remiss in going to church, but if her baby were to live, she would return to her faith and attend church regularly. My heart broke for her. I gently helped her up, hugged her, and guided her back into bed. We both just sat there, holding hands, lost in despair. Words seemed so useless."

"Later on that afternoon, the doctor entered the room with a look of astonishment on his face. He reported that the respiratory problem had disappeared and the baby was going to make it. The doctor couldn't believe it any more than we could. LeRoy? Do you believe it?" Ron asked.

"I believe it, Ron," I spoke quietly. "The Lady is interceding for you to her Son. She is repaying you for all you have done for her. Like Vic said, 'Whoever works on this statue, the Lady will take care of.'"

That afternoon when Ron returned from seeing Mary, he reported that the yellow jaundice had also disappeared from the baby. Relief flooded his face, and he was a happy man again.

Ed Monahan came into the welding shop to report that his brother, Joe, from Washington, D.C., was visiting Butte. After Joe Monahan talked to Roberts, he turned up at the welding shop. He was impressed with the beauty of the statue.

"I'm on the last section now, Joe," I said. "She's just about ready to go on the mountain. How's the helicopter coming?"

"Pretty good," Monahan reported. He recounted the details about the red tape that he, Melcher, and Kimmet had begun to unravel.

"Sounds as if you have been working as hard there as we have here," I said.

"When I talked to Roberts, he wasn't convinced he wanted the army to do it because of the cost," Monahan stated. "I suggested it would cost just as much somewhere else. The lift could be used as a military training exercise for the army, but they aren't certain they can lift it from the yard. The statue may have to be trucked to Elk Park and be lifted from there."

"I sure hope that doesn't happen. I'm not sure the skin will hold up if we have to truck it to Elk Park. The hand section is fifty feet wide,

and the lowboy is only eight feet wide. All the rest would be overhang!" I said
thinking of the problem. "Barker's a good transport driver, but I don't think he's hauled anything that wide. If the rings get bent, we'd never get them bolted together. Nothing would fit. Keep your fingers crossed, and keep working on it."

I decided to let Mary handle that problem too. She knew the best way to accomplish getting to the summit of the mountain. I wonder how long it would be before she let us know?

Ron notified me he had found a job in Hawaii and would be leaving soon. I felt it was unfortunate he had to leave before the statue was completed, but I understood that he had to support Mary and the baby now. Expressing how I would miss him, I also conveyed my feelings of the Lady still taking care of him by finding him this job. After Ron talked with Joe Roberts, he felt better about leaving. Because he was soon to be gone, Ron decided to show Randy Wixten how to run the wire welder. When I checked on him, Randy was welding with cutting glasses instead of the welding hood. I jumped all over him for it, exclaiming he was going to hurt his eyes and burn his face.

"Ron welds like this," Randy explained.

"I know he does," I said loudly, "but he wears a beard!" Randy felt if Ron could do it, he could be macho and do it, too. I could see it was futile in talking to Randy. At the end of the day, I looked at Randy. Boy, was his face red! I just shook my head, and had all I could do to say, "I told you so!" After a few days, he looked like a raccoon. His face had started to peel and he looked awful.

"I wish I had listened to you, LeRoy. I thought sunburns hurt, but this is worse," Randy admitted finally. Ron certainly left an indelible memory for Randy.

Mike Cerise and Bill Fisher were anticipating going to the mountain, but a compressor still hadn't been found. Roberts had approached everyone in town about a compressor, but all were being used. He had even thought about buying one at an auction, then selling it when we no longer needed it. So far, none had materialized. One day while talking to my daughter, Cindy, I mentioned we were trying to acquire a compressor. Later that evening, her husband, Del Snyder, called and recalled seeing one at MHD, where he was employed. The next day, after informing Joe about the compressor, he immediately called out there. At first they refused him, but later in the day, they had a change of heart, and offered Roberts the use of the compressor for the Lady. Joe instructed me to pick up the compressor from the MHD yard and bring it to Roberts' yard.

What a surprise! The compressor was like new! When I saw it didn't have a coupler on it, I put a bolt in it. Being able to go only twenty miles per hour, I took all the back roads. The compressor kept swaying back and forth without much control, so when a car came, I pulled over to the side to let it pass. The first thing I did upon arrival at Roberts was to inform Joe of the instability of the compressor. I recommended they install a coupler on it before they attempted to bring it on the mountain.

Now that Ron was gone, work on the statue wasn't progressing as fast as we would hope. One of the machinists asked Joe if he could give his stepson a job working on the statue. When Joe asked my opinion, all I wanted to know was if he could weld. Joe thought he was able to stick weld, but wasn't sure he could wire weld. We decided to let him volunteer for awhile since we really needed the help. I let him weld for awhile, then went to talk to Joe. When Joe asked me my opinion about Rick working, I mentioned he would learn to weld on the job. Ron had, so did Vic, and both of them have become quite good at it. On the way back to the shop, I had to chuckle to myself. This was more like a welding school than a place of business! I started Rick on the inside of the statue, double welding the skin. I was pleased to have someone working steadily on the statue again. Now we should have the statue done by fall. He wasn't Ron, but he was a good worker, and hopefully a quick learner.

I got myself in trouble with Roberts again. Last week a reporter came to talk to Joe, and then he came in the welding shop. He asked where the man building the statue was. He caught me at a bad time, and I became quite angry. I told him the whole story and how I came to be building the statue. He asked what I would be most proud of when the statue was done. My answer was "to know that I did it for the people of Butte and in later years I can look up and tell my grandchildren that I built it." When Joe saw the report in the paper, he stormed down to the shop.

"Don't talk to any more reporters!" he screamed at me.
"Why?" I asked, innocent of what he was getting at.
"Because it sounds as if you were the only one who worked on the statue!" Joe was still speaking at the top of his voice.

"Joe, every man who worked on the statue, road, site, or whatever, can look up someday and say I helped build that!" I was getting a little hot under the collar myself by this time. Joe stomped out of the shop and headed towards the office. One thing about Joe, he'd get mad, and I mean MAD! But in a few hours he would get over it. He came down and talked to me afterwards like nothing had happened. Later, I told Pat that I couldn't say anything without getting in trouble. She agreed, and said I never did know when to keep my mouth shut. As she was laughing, I called Bob to see what his opinion was on the newspaper article. He, too, laughed and said that Joe had already called him about the article. Bob had told Joe that he had liked it.

We put the last section on. Three legs fit, and the other one was off by one inch. Joe became upset with it, but I explained that when the statue had been dropped, one leg had gotten out of alignment. It hadn't shown up until we reached the bottom. All I had to do was cut the bracket and move it back into alignment. Joe was pleased with the minor adjustment.

MHD called to reclaim their compressor that was being used on the mountain. When Bill Barth brought it down, you could tell he was unhappy. They only needed it for another week.

"How come it's taking you so long?" I asked Barth.

"You try digging four holes six to seven feet wide and fifteen feet deep in solid rock!" Barth stated, becoming agitated. "Beavis and Issacson blast out the holes and then we dig them out with the jackhammer. That's why we need that air compressor."

Monday, when I returned the compressor to MHD, I found one of the bosses and put the question to him about needing the compressor back. He explained their other one had broken down and this one was to be used as a backup. When I related we only needed it for another week, he suggested I go in the office and talk to them about the problem.

I did --- from office, to office, to office. Finally, someone in charge investigated and found out the broken compressor had been fixed. We would be able to use the compressor for another week. When Roberts and Barth saw me coming into the yard pulling the compressor behind me, they were delighted.

Since there wasn't any vehicle available to return the compressor to the mountain, I volunteered to pull it with my Chevy Blazer. On reaching the upper gate, I found I couldn't open the lock. Someone had installed a new one, and I didn't have the right key. Knowing Barth was coming soon, I just sat and waited for him. Two hours later, he showed up. I was not too happy, to say the least. Barth explained where he wanted the compressor. I had to pull it down a hill and the weight of it pushed me into a big steel tool box. Getting out to see what damage had been done, I was dismayed to find the back side of my Blazer had been pushed in from the compressor. Barth felt bad.

Bill Barth standing in nine-foot hole for the base

    Even Roberts had his problems when he attempted to go to the site. The Butte Mining Museum had a promotional gift to honor the one-millionth person to walk through their gate. A ride to the site of Our Lady was given to the winner. Joe decided to escort the people to the site himself, but neglected to check the fuel tank. Imagine the surprise of all involved when halfway up, the vehicle ran out of gas! Not only was Joe embarrassed, but everyone had to walk down from the mountain. The people on vacation didn't get to the site, Joe had to apologize, and everyone had a long walk out. I bet those people never forget Joe, Butte, and Our Lady in the future. But, as I've said, everyone had their problems and their laughs working for Our Lady!

CHAPTER TWENTY-NINE

OUR LADY PROVIDES A HELICOPTER

Bill Barth came searching for me to ask if I knew any welders willing to work Saturday on the mountain. The foundation for the base needed to be welded enabling them to pour the cement. I volunteered my services, then headed for the telephone to see who might be available. Randy Wixten, eager for the opportunity to work at the site, cancelled his plans for the weekend so he could go. Wally Lindquist, a friend and neighbor, agreed to work also. The next morning, we gathered at Roberts in order to go up at the same time. Randy drove the squirt crane, but halfway up the mountain, the fuel pump went out. The others continued in their trucks while I hurried to my house to call Roberts. He was at home when I informed him of the problems we were having. Because it was Saturday, the machinists weren't working, but Joe promised to get someone to help us. After returning to the location of the squirt crane, I waited only a short while before Jack Guinane showed up with another fuel pump. The road was steep and the squirt crane was still experiencing problems and began heating up. Remembering that the old red truck (called Big Red) was on the top of the mountain, I drove up to get it. We hooked the crane to Big Red and hauled it to the top of the hill, but were then faced with descending the backside of the mountain with severe switchbacks in the offing. Hooking onto the back of the crane, we lowered it and walked it down slowly. On one of the switchbacks, we had a problem and almost turned the crane over. We all breathed a sigh of relief when we managed to reach the top of the hill in one piece.

Advancing towards one of the welders, Bill Barth issued a warning to me concerning its safety. Ed Skubitz had gotten hurt from it the other day. The governor wasn't working properly, causing the machine to run ineffectively. As Ed was trying to remedy the situation, his fingers came in contact with the fan. He was very fortunate he didn't lose his finger. All he suffered was a few broken bones and lacerations.

Leaving there that evening, we all knew we had worked hard. Bill Barth, a hard taskmaster, kept us hopping because he knew we wouldn't be able to return. He had tried to persuade Roberts to let me work on the mountain with them, but Joe wanted the statue completed. I told Barth a young man had come to help on the statue, but he was leaving for the Navy in two weeks. Barth was adamant in wanting my services on the hill, even when I insisted Dan was capable of burning holes in the two-inch plate for the round to go through. Finally, when Barth realized Roberts was not going to allow me on the mountain, he consented to let Dan do the work. When I next saw Barth, he had a smile on his face, and said, "You were right. Dan did a good job!"

Joe conveyed some good news. Joe Monahan had called to divulge a meeting with John Melcher, Barry Goldwater, Stan Kimmet, himself, and the Secretary of Defense, Casper Weinberger. An order had been signed allowing us to use a military helicopter for the airlift. The only drawback would be to reimburse the fuel and the crews living expenses while they were in Butte. It was estimated to be approximately fifteen hundred dollars per hour, totaling around forty thousand dollars in all. Joe Monahan had called his mother Rose to report the good news instead of calling Joe Roberts; she had been the one to ask him for the favor. Being that this was a statue for all mothers, Joe felt it fitting to tell his mother the good news first.

A great relief was experienced by all involved. We had been worried we were going to have to haul each section by truck. A few months earlier, Roberts had me accompany one of the house movers to the site to see if it were feasible to transport the sections by truck He didn't claim it was impossible, but we would have to make the road wider. Each section would have required a couple of days' work. Then there was the problem of finding a crane large enough to position all the sections on top of each other. Getting a helicopter solved so many of the problems. We were all excited!

Not long after, we were on the mountain working on the foundation of the base. Clouds had moved in and we were not able to see very clearly. Sounds of a large vehicle drifted up to us as we were working. I rushed to the edge of the mountain and couldn't believe what I was seeing! It was a huge Mack dump truck and behind it was another one just as large!

"Hey, Randy!" I yelled. "Come here! You won't believe this!" As Randy and I stood there, we saw them approach the switchbacks. The truckers would drive forward to the first switchback, put the trucks in reverse, and back up to the next switchback. They zigzagged back and forth up the steep road, while Randy and I watched in amazement. The truckers had a lot of ingenuity to make it up the ten switchbacks that adorned the steep hillside. Barth had also come over to watch the spectacle of the dump trucks.

"I thought they were going to bring cement trucks," I remarked to him as we stood there watching.

"Mike Cerise brought Ted Farrow from Pioneer Concrete up, but he thought the switchbacks and the sixteen percent grade was too steep for the cement trucks. He offered us his portable plant to mix the cement in," Barth answered me.

"How big is it, and how do you expect to get it up here?" I asked, taken in by the whole project.

"It's on wheels, and Farrow thinks we can get it up with the help of a "Cat." Those trucks are Ray Laslovich's. Mike Cerise employed him do some contracting in Anaconda and convinced him to examine the road. Ray enjoyed the idea of a challenge and offered the use of his trucks to haul the sand, gravel, and bags of cement. Ray and his son are getting paid for driving the trucks up here, but the use of the dump trucks is donated. Roberts felt that was fair, as the rental of dump trucks is quite high, if you can even find them," Barth remarked.

When the trucks had got to the top and had been unloaded, I went over and talked to Nick.

"Some road, huh?" I said to him.

"i guess!" Nick answered. "How come they didn't come across the mountain with the road? Boy, it's a slow process bringing up eight yards of sand and gravel with all those switchbacks and the road being so steep. My dad has taken on some dandies, but this one takes the cake!"

I laughed, and asked where they were hauling the sand and gravel from.

"It's coming from Pioneer Concrete on Maryland Street," Nick answered. "I guess we're supposed to bring up the concrete, too."

We were lucky to get the concrete. A few weeks ago we had gone to Ideal Cement Company. in Trident, Montana, to pick it up. The company was on strike and wouldn't permit the semi-truck through the gate. When we explained to the men picketing that the company had donated twelve hundred sacks of cement to the statue being built in Butte, the men opened the gate, and even helped load the truck. We unloaded the sacks at Roberts Equipment Co., so they would have to be picked up there.

Later Barth approached me about working Saturday on the base. Not knowing what plans had been made, I promised I would try; but if I was unable, I would find someone else who could weld. That evening was our regular mixed bowling league, and we were bowling against John "Hoot" Gibson and his team. Hoot was a self-employed ironworker and expressed how beautiful the Lady was. Never one to miss a chance to get workers, I asked Hoot if he would like to help with her. Hoot wasn't available for Saturday, but he promised he would be there Sunday. I still needed someone for Saturday, so I called my son-in-law, Del Snyder. When we arrived at the site, we found the welder still was not operating properly. We put a piece of wood in the governor so it would run open. After operating that way for some time, it just quit, and would not run anymore. When I went home, I called Hoot to see if he had a welder we could use. Hoot was glad to help out. When he came the next day to help, he brought another 220 welder, just like the other one. They worked beautifully, and Hoot let us use them for as long as we needed them. With the good help and the use of the welders, we accomplished what we set out to do that weekend.

Joe inquired if I knew where we could solicit some large tanks. We needed them to hold water used for mixing cement on the mountain. The airport had donated a 5,000 gallon truck to transport the water to Elk Park. From there they would transfer the water to the Search and Rescue's 1,000 gallon truck, which was already in Roberts yard, and the donated Rocker Fire Department truck. Those two trucks would transport the water to the top of the mountain to fill the tanks which Pete Tallon was to bring up with his four wheel drive truck. The problem was to find more large tanks. We scrounged around until we had ten 500 gallon tanks. Joe directed me to weld the tanks together to form one large tank. That way we would only have to fill up one tank and the water would filter into the other ones. This had to be done on top of the mountain before the water could be transported.

When I arrived to weld the tanks together, Paul Tallon and Bob Jelich were there with Pete who had just brought the tanks up. Noticing the bandage on Jelich's finger, I inquired about his finger. Last week when we were putting the beams down for the base, Jelich got his finger caught under one. The beam weighed over a ton and we all thought he lost his finger. When he unwrapped the bandage, I couldn't believe how good it looked. It was almost healed. The Lady sure does take care of the people who work for her!

Randy and I had finished with the tanks when Barth and the others announced they were heading down the mountain. We volunteered to lock the gate when we were done loading our equipment. On the way down, we met Ray Laslovich and his son, Nick. Nick jumped out of his truck and came running over to us.

"Hey, LeRoy!" he shouted, "we've got over 400 sacks of concrete on these trucks. How about giving us a hand?"

"How come you're coming up so late?" I quizzed him, not too happy with the prospect of unloading 400 sacks of concrete.

"We couldn't find anyone to run the forklift at Roberts and it took us until now to get here," Nick replied.

"Did you ask Barth and the others to help?" I asked hopefully.

"We did, but they said you and Randy were still here and would help. Then they took off down the road," Nick said.

Reluctantly, Randy and I went back and helped them unload the two trucks. We didn't finish until after dark. Later, Nick and his father thanked us all the way down the mountain.

I gave it a lot of thought and figured there must be a better way to unload all those sacks of cement. We still had eight hundred to go and that's a lot of work unloading them by hand. The next morning I made a sling to go under the pallets the cement was on. Randy and I loaded it into a truck and brought it to the mountain. It started to rain as we drove up the mountain road; when we reached the top, the rain had turned to snow. The sling I had made worked super. We used the small crane and lifted the cement out of the dump truck. Paul Tallon had made a big pot of chili. When lunchtime came, we all enjoyed it immensely as we were cold and hungry. The snow was really coming down later in the afternoon. It was early for this time of the year, as it was only the first week of September. Because of the snow, Nick asked if Randy and I would bring Big Red down and help him up the steep hill if he needed it. There was more snow on the hill than we expected. We pulled Nick up part of the way and then had to winch him the rest. It's a good thing we followed him down the mountain road. He would never have made it, otherwise.

Barth had a friend who was going to tear down his garage. He thought it would be a good idea to bring it to the top of the mountain as a shelter for the men working there. Randy and I were working on the site when Barth asked us if we'd bring Big Red down to help them with the garage. The hill was muddy and the trailer with the garage on it was heavy. Pete tried, but couldn't hold the trailer back. It slid down the road, hitting a big rock. If it hadn't hit the rock, Pete and the truck might have gone over the bank.

When we stopped for a minute, I asked Earl Casagranda how they were able to get the garage through the tunnel where the road passed through. He stated they flattened the tires, and then it just barely fit.

We hooked Big Red to the trailer and it wasn't too bad until we reached the switchbacks. Pete's four wheel drive didn't have the power to get around the switchbacks, so Randy would take Big Red and winch him up.

Big Red winching the truck hauling the garage up the steep road

"Leave it here," Earl suggested, as the road was going to get rougher. We all agreed except for Barth.

"No, we'll get it up there," Barth insisted.

Randy was pulling with Big Red when the cable came off. Down the hill went the trailer and garage. As I watched the whole contraption going down the hill, I thought, "That's the end of that! When the trailer hits that switchback, it will go over the bank!"

But it went half way and stopped. We couldn't believe it! So we tried it again. We kept telling Barth that the Lady didn't want it up there.

"It'll make it! You watch!" Barth repeated over and over.

We made it through seven switchbacks and then the garage slipped off the trailer.

"Let's leave it," Earl said disgustedly.

"NO," Barth said, determined to accomplish what he set out to do. "Let's get it back on the trailer." Earl looked at Barth with astonishment, shook his head, and went inside the garage to help lift it back onto the trailer. Somehow, the floor trapped his leg and he started to holler loudly. If the garage moved, it would break his leg. I ran in, grabbed a plank, and lifted it up, enabling Earl to free his leg. We all just sat there trying to make Barth give up the project.

"She doesn't want it up there, Bill," Earl said emphatically. The rest of us agreed and tried to get Barth to listen to reason.

"If it's the last thing I do, I'm going to put this garage on the mountain!" Bill said, not listening to anyone. Just then, Big Red, --- which was in front of the garage --- jumped out of gear and plummeted into the garage. The wall went out and roof fell in with a cloud of dust settling all around it. We were stunned! We didn't know what to make of it.

"Bill," I said, "we told you she didn't want it up there." We had to laugh. Mary couldn't have made it more clear what she wanted.

"Well, maybe not the garage, but the roof is still good," Barth stated, not giving in if he could help it --- not even to the Lady. Then we took the roof and set it aside out of the way.

"We didn't get it all here, but Barth should be happy that some of it is here," laughed Earl.

It was time to bring the portable cement plant in from Boulder, Montana, a town about forty miles away. Dave Barker was selected as the lucky man to drive a loader to help pull the plant up the switchbacks. It seemed like we had to pull or push everything up and down that mountain. The Lady didn't want this to be an easy job. Once the plant was in place, Rod Farrow set up the batch plant while Barth was placing the rebar with the help of John Shea and Earl Casagranda. Tom Holter read off the color coded design from the blueprints. Barth made sure each piece went in the right place. He also had help from Pete Tallon,

Bob Jelich, Jim Keto, Ed Stepan, and Art Gerry. As the rebar was put in, Randy and I welded them in place. Bob O'Bill and Mike Telling ran copper wire from the foundation down to a spring in an old mine so that if it got hit by lightning, nothing would get hurt. We were almost ready to pour the base. All we needed were more workers. We were sure Mary would supply them when the time came.

CHAPTER THIRTY

THE BIG POUR

Joe Roberts and Bob O'Bill had publicized that the pour for the foundation was to take place on September 14. On arriving that crispy morning at Robert's yard, I noticed twenty-five men had shown up. After a breakfast of doughnuts and coffee, the group proceeded to the mountain site. As Barth and I were driving up, he mentioned his sister, Lorraine Childs. Lorraine and her husband, Art, wanted to assist in some way with the Lady. Even though Art was retired and money was scarce, Lorraine volunteered to provide the food for the men working on the cement pour. Knowing there would be many men to feed, Lorraine was perplexed as to where the money or food would come from. Being a strong Christian, she opened her arms and looked to heaven, saying, "Well, Lord, you did it with the fish and the bread. I could sure use your help now."

Taking the small amount of money she had earned babysitting, Lorraine Childs bought a ham to be sliced for sandwiches. Lorraine called each of her many friends, asking for help with the food and the preparation of it. Never had Lorraine seen such an outpouring of generosity. People came to her door in streams, donating money, food, and asking to help in any way. Donations came from all over the community. A Protestant minister appeared at the door with bread, doughnuts, and fruit. Pasties (a meat pie) were donated from Nancy's Pastie Shop. Pork chop sandwiches from John's Pork Chop Shop and food from all over the city made this a true community project showing the support they felt for the statue. A tremendous community spirit developed among the workers and the donators which still flourishes today.

As Barth and I approached the top of the mountain, I was amazed at the turnout of men congregated there. About seventy men from all walks of life had assembled to help pour cement: business men, police officers, laborers, insurance salesmen, you name it. They were there representing the diverse community of Butte. The white-collar workers had the pleasure of opening twelve hundred sacks of cement into the bucket. Ed Skubitz, operating the crane, swung the bucket of cement and dumped it into the mixer. Mike Cerise, operating the loader, poured the sand and gravel into the batch plant. Rod Farrow then mixed everything together. The two cement trucks, donated by Ted Farrow, would back up to the batch plant, have the mixed concrete loaded into them, then proceed to the base forms to unload.

Pouring the cement into the base of foundation

Bob O'Bill, Bill Barth, and I jumped on the first cement truck to leave the batch plant. Bob O'Bill had a plan to grab Bill Barth's hat and toss it into the first pour. If he was unable to grab the hat, I was to try for it. Barth had that hat from the first day he started on the project, and it had become his favorite. As they made the first pour, Bob reached over to Barth, quickly snatched the hat from his head, and flipped it into the bottom of the base. The hat instantly became part of the base with tons of concrete pouring over it.

143

"I wore that hat from the time we started," Barth shouted at him, startled as he watched his hat disappear from his sight. "That was my favorite hat, too!"

"I know! I'll buy you a new one," Bob laughed at the stunned look on Bill Barth's face. Everyone laughed because Barth still looked like he had lost his best friend. I threw a penny into the mixture for good luck. Joe Roberts searched his pockets for something to throw in, but he came up empty. Finally, one of the fellows handed him a coin so he could leave his mark in the base, too.

At lunch that day, we feasted like kings at God's table. Pete and Paul Tallon had cooked hot food, and with all the food sent up from Lorraine Childs' helpers, we had more than enough. The Lord had indeed multiplied the fishes and bread for her workers.

All day long we had been threatened with storm clouds. We watched the clouds flow towards us, but then they would separate with half bearing south, the other half bearing north. It was the strangest thing we had ever observed. It would rain on both sides of us, but not a drop on the mountain while we were making the pour. The workers breaking open the cement sacks probably could have used some moisture to refresh them. When I walked over to see how things were progressing, I had to laugh. They were so shrouded with cement dust, I couldn't identify who they were until they spoke. Joe Lee, an Undersheriff, and Bob LeCoure, an insurance agent, were indistinguishable, but still maintained their sense of humor. They had dubbed themselves "The Baggers." One guy was so concealed that when I asked who he was, they all laughed.

"Would you believe that is Turtle Johnson, one of our police officers? He should go undercover in that disguise."

As the day came to an end, we had poured 180 yards of concrete, mixed 1200 sacks of cement, and used 9,000 gallons of water. Each hole with the four anchor bolts and rebar in them took 15 yards of concrete each. It had taken us eight hours to put in a base that weighed 425 tons.

As the volunteer cement finishers troweled the cement, I remarked to Joe Roberts, "It's too bad we don't have a plaque to put in the base."

"Run down to the shop and make one up," Joe Roberts remarked on the spur of the moment.

One of the men drove me to the shop and I quickly sketched a picture of Mary on a plate of iron and cut it out. Taking stainless steel rod, I welded these words on the plate:

Our Lady of the Rockies
Started 12-29-79
Base poured 9-14-85
A Dream Come True

When we returned to the mountain site, we started to situate the plaque into the cement. Then someone noticed that a mistake had been made in the date. Feeling bad, I searched until I found a piece of scrap iron. It was rusted, but I cut it anyway and wrote the right date on it. We inserted the plaque into the cement.

LeRoy Lee putting the plaque in concrete base

Feeling the need to be alone, I refused a ride down with one of the fellows. On the trudge down the side of the mountain, I thanked God for the beautiful day we had just had. The reality of the statue soon to be on the mountain overwhelmed me and I needed this time to be with my God and the tremendous feelings I was experiencing.

The next day we returned to the mountain to tidy up the mess and bring the tanks down. Bob O'Bill inquired about the plaque that I had made the mistake on. At first I told him I threw it over the bank; but when I realized he was serious about wanting it, I salvaged it from the scrap in the welding truck. Bob O'Bill grabbed the plaque and placed it in his truck. Barth and I had to laugh. I decided to play a trick on Bob. I told him Joe Roberts wanted it for himself. Bob O'Bill's response was to let Roberts try to get it from him. I realized how serious Bob was in keeping the plaque, so I told him I was just kidding. Bob still maintained that no one was going to take the plaque from him, no matter what.

Joe Roberts hired some people to sandblast the statue so we could paint it. It was more like pressure washing it. I asked if the statue would rust from the water, but they reassured me that the solution had rust preventative in it. It was guaranteed to last for a couple of weeks. The solution produced a tremendous mess all around the statue.

When the time came to remove the wooden forms from the cement base, Randy Wixten, Bill Barth, Earl Casagranda, and I went up on the mountain. When I cut the bolts from the forms to remove them from the cement, Earl Casagranda suggested to Bill Barth that the wooden forms would make walls for the garage we were unable to get to the top of the mountain. Earl started building the garage while Randy Wixten, Bill Barth, and I took Big Red down to bring the roof to the site. Because the wooden forms were circular for the base, the walls of the garage looked like crescent moons, bending in towards the center. We all laughed because no one had ever seen a building of that shape before. I had an old wood stove that I donated to the garage so the workers could be warm when the weather turned cold. While Barth and I went to procure the stove, Earl Casagranda stayed to work on the building. When we returned, Earl had the ends attached and was mending the roof. Barth helped Earl put plywood on the walls, then they black papered it. Finally, we were able to put the stove into the shelter. Earl stood back surveying the work that had been done. He gazed at it fondly, then named it "The Gingerbread Shack."

Pete Tallon was so taken by the whole project that he extended his vacation from California until the pour for the base had been completed. Now to show his appreciation to the workers, he wanted to host a dinner in their honor. He received permission from Joe Roberts, and with the help of his brother, Paul, he rented the McQueen Club for the event. During the evening, Bob O'Bill stood up to introduce each and every man that was there. When Joe Roberts was asked to give a speech, he declined saying, "I'm leaving it all up to Bob to say what has to be said."

I loved it. Bob has always gotten away from speaking, but now he was in the spotlight. Bob did an excellent job. As everyone left, they expressed their thankfulness to the Tallon Brothers for the dinner held in their honor.

Thank God for Vic Duran. He has been changing his shifts so he can weld on the statue every day. My two other workers, Rick and Dan, had moved on to other ventures elsewhere. Bill Barth, now that the base on the mountain was completed, wanted to learn to weld. Barth had gone to a welding school and knew a little about welding, so I started him welding gussets for the statue. Poor Barth! He would keep coming to ask me to look at his welds, which resembled grapes hanging down from a vine.

"Would you put a weld over it so it won't look so bad?" Barth would ask me. When I was done, Bill just shook his head. "It looks so easy when you do it, LeRoy."

"Barth, I've been welding for years. You just started. You keep trying and I'll come back and clean up whenever you need me," I tried to reassure him. I was impressed with Bill Barth. No wonder the Lady chose him. He has a heart of gold and gives one hundred percent no matter what is asked of him.

Laurien Riehl came down and suggested I put more screen into the folds of the veil. He felt they needed to be larger and we needed more of them. As we were talking, Barth came over. We got on the subject of the little statue I was using as a model for the large one. One of them asked why the bent knee on the little one was on the right side, whereas the big statue had the left knee bent. I expressed my feelings that I felt the ninety-foot statue should be different instead of exactly like the ten-inch statue. The conversation then turned to putting the statue together on the mountain.

"I don't think we should try and put the statue together on the mountain," Barth stated.

"How come?" I asked him, curious at his statement.

"With winter coming on, we won't be able to finish it. It will have to stand all winter like that," Barth answered.

"We've got the helicopter coming," I said.

"What we should do is clear a spot and set the pieces behind the spot reserved for the statue; then in the spring, put the statue together with a crane," Barth responded.

"I think Barth's right," said Riehl. "That way you'd have all summer to get it secured."

"You may be right, but I don't think there is enough room to put all the massive pieces up there," I replied.

When Joe Roberts came down later in the day, I repeated what Barth and Riehl thought about putting the pieces on the mountain, but not on top of each other. Joe became angry and stated, "LeRoy, if the statue doesn't go on the mountain now, it never will." Roberts had just returned from Great Falls and by his manner, I could tell something was definitely wrong.

"I may as well tell you," he said. "Roberts Rocky Mountain has just gone bankrupt, and we are now in Chapter 11. This means we have to get reorganized and I feel I can still save the place. But that statue has to be up on the mountain, all together when the helicopter leaves."

I was in a state of shock. Maybe that's why he wants to put the statue up. He was afraid that if he lost Roberts, he would put the statue in jeopardy, too. Still, thinking back over the twenty years I had worked for Joe, the business had been in danger of going under a number of times. I kept thinking of what Joe had said;" If the statue didn't go up now, it never will," Then I wondered if Joe was worried about his cancer and was thinking if the statue didn't go up now, maybe he wouldn't be around to see it go up next year. I couldn't see the Lord doing that because of all Joe had done for His Mother.

CHAPTER THIRTY-ONE

THE MOUNTAIN IS BLESSED

In October of 1985, Father DiOrio was scheduled to speak at the Civic Center. Father DiOrio is a Catholic priest who travels extensively, speaking about the compassion of our Lord. Many healings have taken place during and after his speaking engagements. One of my friends, Dottie Sullivan, had given her testimony concerning Father DiOrio's appearance in Spokane, Washington. Dottie is the mother of seven children, all born within a span of eight years. After the birth of her twins, she developed phlebitis in both her legs. Dottie had veins stripped in her legs, but her left leg had swollen to twice its normal size. After months of intense pain, she was flown to Seattle. There, her left leg was amputated in order to save her life. Her right leg continued to plague her with blood clots, arthritis had developed in her knee from the unexpected demand of having one leg, and her remaining leg was in danger of being amputated also. When her cousin informed her of the healings taking place wherever Father DiOrio spoke, Dottie prayed she would be able to endure the trip to Spokane. Dottie Sullivan was unable to walk or to even sit for any length of time, so she was situated in a prone position in the back of a station wagon all the way to Spokane. Upon her arrival at the auditorium, she was placed in a wheelchair and pushed to the front where she would have a good view of the program. During the services, Father DiOrio walked over to where Dottie was sitting in her wheelchair, asked her how she was and commanded her to walk to him. Dottie dragged her leg a couple of steps, then she walked the twenty feet to where Father was standing. She couldn't believe she was doing this. Father DiOrio instructed her to push her wheelchair out of there. Dottie did, shouting all the way up the aisle, "God loves me!"

After hearing Dottie Sullivan's story, I was anxious to attend the program at the Civic Center. For two days, the Civic Center, which held over six thousand people, was filled to capacity. God's presence was overpowering. Many people experienced spiritual and physical healings. I was happy that I didn't miss this event, even though I had been tempted to.

The next day, Sister Mary Jo McDonald telephoned me at work. Joe Roberts had agreed to take Father DiOrio to the top of the mountain, and she had requested that I accompany him. I approached Joe with the idea, but he was against it, and I was to remain at the shop and work on the statue. I would have loved to have gone with this wonderful man just to talk to him. Just as I was accepting the idea of not being able to go, Joe entered the shop saying they needed another vehicle to take everyone to the mountain. Seeing my chance to go, I volunteered to bring my four wheel drive Eagle. On the way up the mountain, Sister Mary Jo confided they had informed Joe Roberts that Father DiOrio wished specifically to meet LeRoy Lee. I was impressed. I thanked her many times. I was excited to be with this holy man for awhile. As we drove up, snow was drifting down. The huge flakes were beautiful, but everyone expressed their apprehension about the road since it began snowing heavily. The snow gusted all the way and I kept reassuring them the storm would stop when we reached the summit. As we neared the top of the mountain, sure enough, the snow abated and the sun appeared. Father DiOrio was overcome by the view.

"What beautiful country this is!" Father DiOrio exclaimed. "I can see why the Lady wants to be up here. It's like being on top of the world!"

The Rocky Mountain Continental Divide Range begins far up into Canada and stretches down into Mexico covering the North American Continent. It crosses three different countries. Wouldn't it be something if Our Lady of the Rockies is the geographic center of the mountain range? The water that flows to the east goes down the Missouri River to the Atlantic, and the water that flows to the west goes to the Columbia River and out to the Pacific Ocean.

"Is there going to be a chapel up here?" Father DeOrio asked Joe Roberts. When Joe answered that one was in the long range plans, Father thought a moment, then said, "My mother, brother, and I would like to donate an altar for the church."

"That would be wonderful, Father, but Guy Ossello, the man who donated the land here, has already offered us an altar," Joe Roberts said.

"Then let me bless the spot where the statue of Our Blessed Mother will stand." Father DiOrio advanced to where the base stood. Father not only blessed that spot, but the land surrounding the area. Then he reached out over the edge of the mountain and blessed Butte and the people who lived there.

"Wherever I go," Father stated, "I say Mass, and I will say something about Our Lady of the Rockies. I hope to be back in a few years, and I'll try to bring the Pope with me if it is possible."

As we got ready to leave, I petitioned Father DiOrio to pray over Joe Roberts, who was still suffering from cancer. Father consented, and I walked over to the vehicle where Joe was sitting. When I related to him that Father wanted to pray over him, Joe appeared embarrassed, but didn't protest when I escorted him to where Father was praying. Father DiOrio placed his hands on Joe's head and implored God for the healing of Joe. Afterwards, we all returned to our vehicles and started down the mountain. The snow had disappeared, but it left the road very slippery. With all the mire, we had to drive carefully.

The next morning, I questioned Joe Roberts on whether he had felt anything when Father DiOrio had prayed over him. Joe mentioned that he had gotten warm all over, and that night his stomach jumped all around. When he told his wife, Joanne, she mentioned Father DiOrio should have prayed over his back because of the pain he had been experiencing. He announced his back didn't ache anymore.

Oct. 14, 1985

We needed some plates to make gussets for the inside of the statue. When I mentioned to Joe Roberts that when the Anaconda Smelter was being torn down, I noticed every kind of iron we'd need. Joe instructed me to take Randy Wixten and see what I could talk the Anaconda Company out of. Bill Barth insisted on going when he heard about the iron. We approached the man in charge of the salvaging department and asked him if he would donate some iron for the Lady. The man was generous, and we were able to acquire what plate we needed. On the way out, I noticed some walkway off to the side. An idea came to me, and I mentioned putting walkway around the inside of the statue to Barth. Barth thought the idea was worth merit, so I returned to the man in charge to see what we could come up with. He took me out and showed me what there was. I was surprised at the amount they had.

"Do you need some lights?" he asked. "There are six big ones, and they are worth about six thousand dollars each."

"We don't turn anything down!" I replied, grinning.

We returned with the plates and made another trip to pick up the walkways. Joe Roberts was surprised, but happy over the amount of material we had obtained.

Later, I encountered Bob O'Bill looking mighty unhappy.

"What's up, Bob?" I asked.

"Have you seen the paper, yet?" Bob asked, looking quite irate. "The paper put a cartoon in the editorial page about the statue. It said that we changed our minds and were going to put up a statue of Dennis Washington instead of the Blessed Mother. I guess they figured because Washington bought the Anaconda Company and was planning on opening the pit again, it would be great for Butte and all the people out of work. The cartoon just wasn't in good taste."

I agreed with Bob. Sometimes I wonder about the media. They seem to blow hot and cold too often, without any thought of what or whom they might be injuring.

Bill Barth asked Joe Roberts if I could return to the mountain to accomplish more work on the four-foot base structure. After he consented, Bill and I ascended the mountain and were discussing what needed to be done. I kept looking at the two-inch rod extending out about ten inches from the base.

"How does Laurien Riehl plan on bolting the bottom twelve-foot section on those four two-inch bolts?" I asked Barth.

"Cut the holes bigger," said Barth.

"There isn't enough room on the leg plates." I said. "The only way I can see to do it is if I cut four two-inch plates with holes, bolt them on, and cut the plates off the bottom pipe structure. Then after we fly it up, we'll just weld it on."

"That should work. Just make sure you get the right angle on the pipe," said Barth.

On the return from the mountain, I entered the head and shoulders section to remove a collection of iron to prevent any dead spaces when they painted. Vic and I commenced. It required weeks to remove the unnecessary iron and double weld her. Joe was disheartened over the paint being burned, especially on her face, but it had to be done.

In the meantime, Roberts was becoming impatient about the helicopter. He had contacted Washington and thanked them for their efforts in trying to obtain the helicopter, but he decided to proceed with a private company since the government was unsure whether or not they would be able to help. They persuaded Joe to be more patient. They were still engaged in requisitioning the helicopter. They were waiting for word to come at any time, and they felt Joe would have the helicopter before Christmas. Because the cost would be less, Joe decided to wait until after Christmas to continue his search for a private helicopter.

CHAPTER THIRTY-TWO

GETTING PREPARED FOR THE LIFT

An Army helicopter was discharged from Helena, Montana, to view the site where Our Lady was to stand. From there, the helicopter flew over Roberts Rocky Mountain Equipment yard. Roberts accompanied them, and when they were overhead, Joe leaned out and waved to everyone in the yard. The pilots were scouting the site and the area in which the lift was to take place. They were to report to Nevada with their observations. For the actual lift, the pilots would be in Butte several days later to make their own observations.

On December 16, 1985, Joe Roberts hurried to the shop explaining we were to welcome the pilots at the airport. When I jumped into the car, Bill Barth and Bob O'Bill were already seated and ready to go. On our arrival at the airport, the National Guard crew from Helena were present to greet the crew who were designated to fly the Sikorsky Skycrane helicopter from Nevada. The Helena crew informed us they would confer with us after they were done with their consultations. We departed, and when the Nevada crew flew in, they headed directly to the mountain and landed at the site to do a quick survey of the terrain. Then they flew to Roberts' and landed in the middle of the yard, much to everyone's delight. The weather had been cold, and when the chopper landed, the wind surged bitterly through our bodies.

Craig Albee, from Helena, reported the conditions on the mountain were ideal. If the weather remained like this, they anticipated few problems. The colder the weather, the more lifting power the chopper maintains. We were surprised, as the weather had been below zero for over three weeks. Thinking how miserable it would be for the workers, I hoped it wouldn't remain quite that cold.

"The winds will be over one hundred miles per-hour under the chopper," Craig Albee said. "That means the wind chill factor will be around fifty below. You know that building you have up there?" I looked at Bill Barth, thinking about the Gingerbread Shack.

Albee continued, "Well, the winds will be so strong, they will blow the building over!"

"Hey, Barth," I shouted at him, "you had better nail it down or we won't have a place to eat or get warm."

As we walked around the huge sections of the statue, one of the crew asked me, "Are you sure they will all fit?"

"I hope so," I answered.

"You hope so! You don't know?" He stopped in his tracks and looked at me curiously.

"We've never had them all together, yet," I answered.

"Oh, great! That's all we need is to get up there and it won't fit!" moaned the pilot.

"It'll fit!" shouted Joe Roberts. "It'll fit!"

Albee then remarked he didn't think it was possible to remove the sections from the yard. It would be too dangerous with all the buildings and wires around. Joe was so anxious to comply with all they required that he suggested the statue could be moved to wherever they felt it necessary to lift it from.

As Albee walked around the massive structures he informed us we had to keep the pieces around 15,000 pounds, as they would be going up with only fifteen minutes of fuel. If they encountered trouble where it would be over fifteen minutes, he'd have to place the segment down and return for more fuel. He also specified that if the weather was inclement, (which at this time of the year was almost a certainty), they would leave the helicopter at Bert Mooney Airport, fly back to Nevada with the crew, and return when the weather improved.

"Make sure that no one has any flesh exposed when the chopper is over them, as the winds will freeze their skin immediately," advised Albee. "If we remove the pieces from here, it would lift the roof from your welding shop. That's how strong the wind will be. Have as few men as possible on each post just to guide the section." Looking at Joe Roberts to see how his instructions were being received, Albee then dropped his bombshell. "We are ready to put it up this weekend."

Joe looked stunned. He hadn't expected it to be so soon. He scrutinized my face and questioned, "When will you be ready?"

"Not for a week, yet," I answered, as dazed as Joe.

"O.K." Albee said, "but whatever you do, make sure we can do it. The National Guard doesn't want to bring the Sikorsky Skycrane helicopter in here and have you say you're not ready. Here we'd be with mud on our face. I don't know what kind of power you people have. I saw the letters, and they said you could have the helicopter as long as you wanted it --- now or six months from now. Just make sure you are ready."

"We'll lighten the heavy section and weigh each piece. We'll be ready!" said a smiling Joe Roberts. Then Joe looked at me and said, "We will, won't we? It would be nice to have the statue up before Christmas."

"You told them we would be ready, Joe. I'll make sure we're ready if we have to work night and day!" I grinned back at him. Joe winked and smiled.

"You bet!!" he said.

That night as I was relating what happened to my wife, Pat, doubts crept into my thoughts. "What if they didn't fit?" They had never been all together yet. "What if they really didn't fit?" I expressed my feelings to Pat.

"Don't worry, LeRoy," she reassured me. "The Lady took care of everything so far. She isn't going to let anything happen now. Just turn it over to God and Mary."

Joe Roberts informed me that Ron James from the Ironworkers Union had come down to talk to him. Ron insisted that putting iron together was ironworkers work, and he wanted the ironworkers to put the statue up on the mountain. He felt working under the helicopter was dangerous and because he had men who knew what they were doing, the work should be theirs. Joe stated if they had men who would volunteer their time, then they would be more than welcome to help. We already had John Shea and Tom Holter, but we would accept anyone who felt they wanted to volunteer. Bill Barth was sure to be more comfortable working with men who were experienced ironworkers.

Bob O'Bill asked me if I was able to get welders to help on the mountain during the lift. I told him none of the welders were anxious to work on the mountain because of the extreme cold weather we were experiencing. Bob related the same problem in recruiting men to help. Joe Roberts was not unduly upset. He had reported he would get men on the mountain even if he had to hire them. He always had Bill Barth, Al Beavis, Mike Cerise, Bob O'Connor, Earl Casagranda, John Shea, and Tom Holter. Bob O'Bill reported we had all been together for all these years, and nothing would keep them off the mountain, especially a little cold weather. I replied Mary will see that plenty of men will be up there when we need them.

That evening, a meeting was held at Roberts' office. Around thirty men appeared for the briefing. Bob O'Bill explained to the men how cold it would be on the mountain, how the rotor blades would make the wind chill factor extreme, and how to dress warm to prevent freezing their skin. Joe Roberts volunteered insulated coveralls for any man needing them to keep warm. I suggested that any man who lived in Montana should have enough heavy clothing, but Joe said he would get some coveralls just in case. Joe expressed his determination that no matter how cold it got, that statue was going up on the mountain!! All the men expressed a desire to help, so we had enough men to work the weekend to prepare the statue for her trip up the mountain. Excitement was running rampant throughout the whole city of Butte. Everyone knew they were experiencing history in the making.

Laurien Riehl entered to complain I didn't put large enough bolts in the plates that bolted the structure together. I explained that I used what we had: seven-eighths bolts. Bob had them donated and we didn't have money to buy larger ones. Besides, once we put the four bolts in the plate, then we'll weld around the plate, and that's a lot of weld.

I was ecstatic with the turnout of helpers who came to help prepare the statue. Eighteen men came to help. I put two welders to finish up the rings. Barth took a few to put cross trusses in. Vic was cutting plates to weld on the cross pipes once they were up. Barth was working on a ladder when it collapsed and he plunged to the ground. When the men told me, I couldn't believe it! Barth was Mr. Safety himself. He would get so angry at me because I'd hang by one hand and weld. I was so hyper, I never took time for safety. Hurrying over to the section of statue he was in, I found he smashed his leg on one of the cross pipes.

"You'd better go home, Bill," I said, worriedly. "You're not a young man and you are really hurting."

"NO! I'm staying, but someone else is going up that ladder. I'll hold it," Barth was insistent.

Later I told Vic Duran, "I don't know where Barth gets all his energy. He smokes like crazy, is overweight, but he does the work of two men."

"Thank God we've got him," said Vic.

"That's why Mary picked him," I told Vic.

Joe Roberts journeyed to Missoula for a set of scales which had been donated to weigh each section of the statue. Bill Barth bossed the crew while Dave Barker ran the crane: Tom Holter, John Shea, and other ironworkers took turns getting up on the posts and hooking up the cables to the hook. Once the piece was lifted, Barth would take his transit and determine how much iron Vic and I would have to take out. We couldn't add any more because they were too heavy as it was. Tom Holter told Bill Barth if each piece wasn't level, when the chopper set it down on the following piece, and it hit, the skin would wrinkle. Barth and I agreed that it was a good thing Tom had thought of that, because neither of us had.

CHAPTER THIRTY-THREE

DECEMBER 17, 1985 - DAY ONE OF THE BIG LIFT

The National Guard helicopter was scheduled to arrive at noon but failed to show up. The next morning, Joe explained why he didn't make contact with the crew until that evening. The crew had become disoriented during a blinding snowstorm and had begun to doubt they would ever find Butte. When at last they had arrived, Joe Roberts settled them into the Copper King Inn located near the airport. The crew would be the guests of the Copper King Inn for as long as the lift would take with a rental car at their disposal.

Roberts remarked that they were not the same crew members which had come the last time. The former pilot was unable to pass his physical and had been grounded! Another crew had been chosen and the main crew were due around eight o'clock.

When I saw Bob O'Bill, I was surprised at his appearance. He looked as though he hadn't slept in a week. When I commented on his pallid face, he seemed a little testy.

"Why?" he remarked.

"You look like you've been up all night," I replied.

"I have!" said Bob. "One of the National Guard jeeps went off the road and hit one of the power poles on the mountain, causing a power outage. We worked all night restoring power so you would be able to use the welders today." Bob really did look beat.

"Who were you able to get that late at night, Bob?" I asked.

"Phil Telling and some other electrician. Telling had to climb a tree and free cut some branches to detach the tangled power lines. We got home about 4:00 a.m. It was too late then to go to bed; besides, I was afraid of missing something. After waiting this long, I'm sure not going to sleep while the lift might be taking place," Bob said.

"I know how you feel, Bob. I had one hard time getting to sleep, too. I was so anxious for the lift to start, all I could visualize was all these years of hard work, and it's really about ready to happen!" I said, expressing my anxiety to Bob.

"Where did all these men come from, Bob? I've never seen most of them before," I remarked as I noticed a group of men piling out of their cars.

"They came to help wherever they might be needed," Bob said, as he smiled.

As I stood there watching the flight crew climb out of the van, I thought, "I'll remember December 17, 1985, the rest of my life. Will everything go as we hope? Will someone get hurt? Will the pieces fit together? Will they be able to lift the sections, or will they still be too heavy?"

I was full of excitement and fear. My stomach kept doing flip-flops, and my hyperactive body was in full gear. I couldn't settle down in one spot. It was like waiting to go downstairs on Christmas morning when I was a child.

Bob O'Bill had already welcomed the crew last night at the Copper King Inn with Roberts and Joe Monahan. Roberts called me over and introduced me to the pilot, Marc Comstock. I felt a little nervous at first because I realized this was the man responsible for putting all the pieces of steel on the mountain. What took me five years to build, he would put together in five days!

Pilot Marc Comstock and Co-pilot Bruce Britton

"This is LeRoy Lee," Roberts said presenting me to Marc Comstock. "Lee's the man who built the statue."

I reached out shaking his hand proudly. Then Comstock turned and introduced me to his co-pilot, Bruce Britton and his winch man, Tom Bortner. They had all served in Vietnam together. After shaking each of their hands, I was introduced to the ground crew: Steve Petersen, Hank St. Clair, and Robert Coleman.

Turning to me, Comstock said, "You're going to show us the structure we're going to be flying."

I led them across the yard to where the sections lay waiting for their final resting place on the mountain.

Comstock then asked, "What type of winds will we be dealing with on the mountain?"

"Westerly winds," answered Bob O'Bill.

"West?" said Comstock.

"Yes, that's the direction," Bob said, pointing away from the East Ridge. "They come from the west and go toward the east." Bob had moved in a semicircle and was now pointing to the site where the Lady would be installed.

"We'll be facing Butte, then?" Comstock inquired, setting the locale in his mind.

Bob shook his head yes.

Comstock briefed us thoroughly on the procedure he would be following, from hooking up each section to setting it down. He explained what they wanted, what they thought, and then asked what we wanted and what we could do. His whole manner expressed a man in authority who knew what he was doing. I was reassured the Lady was in very competent hands.

"LeRoy," Comstock said, turning to me, "what is the weight of each section?"

"Barth weighed each section around eight tons. One is heavier than that, though," I replied.

"How heavy?" he asked.

"Nine tons. We took out all the iron we could." I said.

"Well, eight tons is at sea level. I don't know what it will do at this altitude. It should lift more in the cold, though. Well, all we can do is try. We'll forget what the book says and hope for the best," Comstock remarked.

"Do you want one of us to go with you in the helicopter?" Bob asked.

"We can't take anyone unless they are in the service," said Comstock.

Another briefing took about fifteen minutes. When it was over, the crew announced they were departing to the airport. Then they would fly around to become familiar with the conditions before they picked up the first piece. Joe Roberts told them the skirting was cabled and ready to go.

As we walked through the yard, Comstock turned to Joe, pointed at me, said, "I want Lee to go with us. Have him at the airport before eleven o'clock."

WOW! He was talking about me! What an honor to ride in a helicopter of that dimension with a crew like this! I'd never flown in a helicopter before, and a better occasion would never come along. Boy, was I excited! I couldn't believe my luck.

When I arrived at the airport, the crew was getting ready to take off. Up close, the helicopter was enormous. The small chopper looked like a toy along side the Sikorsky Skycrane. Running out to the runway, I was detained by a guard. I pointed at the Sikorsky and shouted that I was expected to get on it. The noise was earsplitting. The guard shook his head and pointed to the small helicopter. Again, I pointed to the Sikorsky, but the guard shook his head and directed me to the little chopper. My face must have shown my disappointment, because the guard relented and said he would find out for sure. He extracted a radio from the side of the plane, conversed for a few seconds, then waved me aboard the Sikorsky. My excitement soared once more.

As I climbed inside the helicopter, Comstock smiled and pointed to a seat in between him and his co-pilot. The seat was situated a little behind them, so I would not be in their way. I settled down and he pointed to a pair of earphones. He handed me a set of earplugs, which I was happy to use to shut out the noise inside the chopper. Next, the earphones went on. Surpisingly, I could hear Comstock quite well.

"Welcome aboard," Comstock said, smiling. "See this handle on my side?" He pointed to the door. I shook my head yes. "If anything happens to this chopper, and I don't open this door, then I'm either hurt or dead. You will have to do it. The same with the co-pilot's door. Understand?"

Again, I shook my head. Excitement was mounting within me at every moment, and I had actually become speechless. This was a first for me! I remember thinking, "Do I really want to do this?" Then my

sanity returned and they couldn't have gotten me out of there for anything.
    We flew to the site, then approached from the back, above the site. I could observe the men waving at us. Comstock made a few passes around the site, commenting on how close the sixty-foot cliff was to the base. He would have to be extremely careful when lowering the first sections, leaving out a lot of cable to prevent the rotor blade of the helicopter from hitting the cliff. Sitting there peering out the window of the chopper, I became aware how dangerous this job was. Flying back down the mountain, I pointed to Highways 15 and 90 and informed Comstock that was the route designated for them to fly over. The police would have the highways closed for all traffic with the exits blocked to keep cars from entering.
    As we approached Roberts' yard, I was surprised. I thought I would be taken back to the airport. Instead, Comstock flew over to the skirting, hovered, and started to lower the hook. Thinking about what the other pilot, Albee, had said about the winds blowing the welding shop roof off, I kept one eye on the building, and one eye on the hook being lowered. One of Comstock's ground crew, Steve Petersen, hurried over and hooked up the cables of the first piece, the skirting. My heart jumped inside of my chest, as I realized I was having the privilege of seeing the first piece brought to the mountain. Excitement raced through me, when I saw the skirting slowly ascending towards the helicopter. I could hardly contain myself, and I had a hard time sitting in the seat. My head was bouncing from one side to the other as I tried to watch the skirting slowly swinging from side to side. Then when it was at the correct level, the helicopter thrust upward and dipped towards the mountain site. At the last minute, I noticed the welding roof. I expected to see it blown away, but it remained intact on the building. Maybe because the section was lifted from the bottom of the yard, the winds weren't quite so severe.
    Comstock took a turn to the south, and I informed him that if he continued to go in that direction, he would be taking the long way because of the housing developments in that area. He decided to change directions and fly over the Berkeley Pit area where few homes were. We approached the site carefully, and Comstock hovered over the base. Slowly he lowered the section to the base. I couldn't believe I had the best seat in the chopper! I could look out of the pilot's and co-pilot's windows, then turn around and watch Bortner, the winch man. When Comstock was certain the section was settled into place, he gave

Bortner, the winch man, the signal and the hook was released. Quickly the helicopter rose, and the cable extending down was brought up inside of the helicopter. We proceeded to the airport where we landed, and my thrilling experience was at an end. As we left the chopper, the crew invited me to lunch at the Airport Restaurant.

Entering the restaurant, we were approached by some very angry policemen. They had gone to a lot of trouble and inconvenience to close the highways and the pilots had chosen another route without telling them. The police felt embarrassed because people were wondering why the highways were closed. Comstock was very diplomatic about the situation. He apologized and informed them they would be taking the railroad tracks from now on. Then if anything happened, they wouldn't be tying up the highways. This appeased the police, who liked the idea of the railroad tracks much better, as this would make traffic control easier.

Sitting in the restaurant, I couldn't help gazing over at the huge Sikorsky sitting at the airport. The thrill of being involved in lifting the first section remained with me. Curious about the aircraft, I questioned the co-pilot, Bruce Britton about the helicopter. He told me it was 26-feet high, 88 feet long, with the rotor blades 72 feet diameter. It consumes 750 gallons of fuel per hour because of its two gas turbine engines which put out 4,500 horsepower.

On hearing this, I remarked, "You sure know your helicopter!"

"I should," he answered, "I've been flying Skycrane since 1980, and have been in the military since 1968."

"What about you, Marc?" I asked of the pilot.

"I've been on Skycrane since 1970, and in the Army since 1966. We feel pretty lucky to be here," Marc Comstock replied. Officers Albee and Terry Alberti were from the original crew that was supposed to be here. They're back in Reno, and we're the ones picked to do the job."

"There must be a reason," I stated.

Comstock was silent for a moment; then he remarked, "This is really a neat project. Many times we lift things that we never see again. This statue will be here a long time. We can come back with our grandchildren and take a look at it, and know we had a part in putting it on the mountain." Everyone agreed with him.

"Well, if I'm going to be on the mountain when you bring up the next piece, I'd better get going," I said, as I started to get up. "I can't thank you enough for letting me go up with you in the helicopter. It was the thrill of a lifetime. Thanks, again."

Sikorsky Skycrane Helicopter

"I want you to do something when you get up on the mountain," Comstock said. "There were too many men on the site when we flew in with the skirting. I wasn't too worried about that piece because it was only four-foot high and weighed two tons. I will be worried about the next section though. Didn't you say it went around eight ton?"

"Yes," I replied.

"I only want enough men to grab the tag lines out there. By the way, how come they had a boom on that building on the site?" Comstock asked.

"That's our Gingerbread Shack," I said. "The other crew said it would blow away because of the wind from the rotor blades." Comstock just laughed.

"I don't think it's that bad," he said, still chuckling.

As I drove up the mountain that afternoon, my thoughts were still filled with the excitement of being on the Sikorsky Skycrane. I wondered if any of the men saw me waving at them and if they knew it was me. Nearing the top of the mountain, I noticed the clouds were really low and were putting the mountain into a deep fog. Some of the men asked how my ride was, but their thoughts were more on the weather than anything. Bob O'Bill had received a message on the portable radio that the airlift was cancelled until the fog cleared. Disappointment was evident on all the men's faces. I asked Randy Wixten if there were any problems with the skirting when they set it on the base. Randy remarked that when they set the skirting on the base with the crane, it had hung up on some of the crossbars. He and Vic had to cut them in order for the skirting to fit.

"Don't worry," Vic retorted. "We took care of your work when you were out flying around."

"Jealousy will get you nowhere," I laughed. "It was sure fun."

We waited for hours for the fog to lift, wondering if we would get the next section today. If we weren't looking over the cliff gazing down below into the fog, we were talking about the chopper and the excitement of the day. Then around two o'clock, the weather started to clear. Bob O'Bill went to his pickup and called down to Roberts' on his CB radio. They had a base station set up down there, and were waiting for the call.

"Hey," Bob shouted over the radio. "It's clearing up here and the wind has died down. How about the other section?"

About an hour later, word came over the radio that the chopper had left Bert Mooney Airport. We all ran to the edge of the cliff to watch the Skycrane head for Roberts' yard. The excitement started to mount again. As we watched, we saw the chopper rising from the yard with the next section attached to its line. One of the men on the mountain had a radio tuned into station KBOW. Connie Kenney was talking about the air lift.

Connie Kenney, announcer for KBOW Radio

As we all listened, we heard her say, "Once again, it's a lift off!" The excitement in her voice echoed what everyone felt down in Butte. Whenever something was about to happen, Connie relayed the play-by-play description to the public. This must be what it's like to cover a shuttle mission.

"Here we go again! So Mountain Men, it's on its way. Going up and up and up! Get ready, Mountain Men!" Connie Kenney let us know each time what was going on down in the city of Butte. We felt privileged because we knew what was happening there and on the mountain. I mentioned to Bob that he was going to have to be our "Connie" and let people down below know what was happening on the mountain. But he didn't hear me; he was already on the CB radio talking to people at Roberts.

As the helicopter drew nearer, a handful of men ran out to grab the long tag lines hanging from the section. The snow, picked up by the rotor blades, was blowing all around us. I was surprised at the wind; it wasn't as bad as they had predicted. Bortner, the winch man, lowered the section slowly as the men on the tag lines kept it from swaying. When it was lowered onto the legs of the four-foot section, the ironworkers put their spud bars in the holes and dropped in the bolts. The helicopter then released the hook. When they flew over the site, we all waved to them as they headed back to the airport. Our work had just begun. I commented to Randy Wixten that I didn't think it was any worse than putting it together with the crane when we put the shoulders on the bust section. He agreed. Randy, Vic Duran, and Jim Keane stayed with me to get the section welded, even though it would be late that evening before we were done. Each of us took a leg and started welding the plates together. Then we attached the gussets. It was quite late when we finished, but we were in no hurry to leave. We all knew we wouldn't be able to sleep after the excitement of the day. I, for one, was totally awake. I didn't want the day to end. It had been a day that would long live in my memories. Since the day had gone so well, I expected the whole lift to be as smooth and without trouble as today had been.

CHAPTER THIRTY-FOUR

DECEMBER 18, 1985 - TOO MUCH WIND

The next morning, December 18, I inquired how everything went at Roberts' yard during the lift. Earl Casagranda and John Shea reported the excitement was almost as intense as it was on the mountain. Earl couldn't refrain from describing the helicopter lifting that massive section. People came in droves to observe the drama taking place. Cars were stopping on the highway, forcing the police to beckon them on. The only regret Earl and the other fellows voiced was that after the section had been removed from the yard, they would like to join the rest of the workers on the mountain top. When asked how many men they had to hook up the section, Earl named the following: Tom Holter, Jack Starin, Henry Ritz, John Miller, Ludie Sustarsic and the two National Guard crew, Sergeants Hank St. Clair, and Robert Colemen.

A meeting involving all the men was called by the pilots at Roberts' office. Comstock expressed his displeasure over the number of men on the mountain.

"There are too many men up there on the site and on the tag lines. I don't want anyone getting hurt. When you're sitting in my seat, and see that structure swinging over the men's heads, it's scary. So from now on, I don't want anyone on that site until the piece is ready to set down."

Everyone agreed with Comstock's advice and we all dispersed for the mountain or to the ground crew.

Bill Barth had taken a crew to the mountain earlier to make sure everything was ready... The pilots had departed for the airport, so Bob O'Bill and I headed for the mountain for another day that would be etched in our memories. Upon reaching the site, I expressed my surprise that the helicopter hadn't been there yet. When I asked Jim Keane, he reported they hadn't radioed to the pilots to bring the next section up yet. Bill Barth was still occupied inside the structure, so I went to find out what he was doing. He had instructed the welders to put in angle iron from the legs to the six-inch channel. I became quite upset.

"What are you putting those in for? We don't need them. Let's get this statue up!" I shouted at Barth, anxious to see the whole structure up as soon as possible.

"We need them for safety for the ironworkers," Barth stated.

"Bill, we've been working and walking on these pipes for five years. Those ironworkers are used to it. They don't need a place to stand." (I was becoming extremely irritated with Barth).

"If we are going to work, let's do it safely." Barth was just as adamant as I was as we stood there facing each other.

"Last week it was twenty-five to thirty below zero. So far we've been lucky. The weather has been above zero. We can't expect this kind of weather to last very long this time of the year. I say we get this statue up, and worry about the places to stand after," I retorted, stomping out of the structure and heading for the Gingerbread Shack, angry with the delay.

Barth burst into the building.

"Where's my lunchbox, Bob?" Barth demanded. "I'm leaving. I just don't want anyone to get hurt."

I experienced unhappiness in letting my anxiety dominate me and yelling at Barth. I followed Barth to where the vehicles were.

"Come on, Bill, don't leave." I started to put my hand on his arm. Barth's anger really exploded then.

"Just stay away from me!" he yelled. "Bob, will you drive me home?"

Bob O'Bill hurried over and indicated to me he would talk to Barth. I retreated to where Jim Keane was standing, still surprised at Barth's blowup. I had never seen Bill angry before. He had always been such a quiet, shy man. Keane explained that emotions were running high from the lift, and no one had been sleeping very well. Barth was just overwrought about someone getting hurt.

I knew I had been wrong. I informed Keane I would make sure the angles would be installed, and left to take care of the matter.

Walking away, I muttered to myself, "I should never have said anything. Bill is right. It's better to be safe than sorry."

After I welded the angles in, I glanced up at the rock on my right side. Nick Daly was installing something on a pole or stick. I asked Vic Duran what Nick was doing. The pilots had asked us to put a wind pylon on top to tell which way the wind was blowing. Suddenly, we were interrupted by one of the men running all over the site, yelling, "Connie Kenney said they're about ready to lift the next section."

We scrambled to the radio and heard her excited voice coming over the airwaves.

"It's Liftoff! Mountain Men, get ready! You've got about a ten minute wait. So once again, liftoff has been accomplished. This is the second piece!"

One of the men said, "I like that. Mountain Men!" So from then on we called ourselves "The Mountain Men."

"I wish the wind wasn't blowing as bad as it is," Bob O'Bill said, after watching the wind pylon stretching out with the wind. "I hope they'll be able to set it down in this wind."

We all watched the wind pylon Nick Daly had installed for signs of the wind letting up a little. We observed the helicopter veer to the south and wondered if he deviated from course because of the strong winds.

"All right," Bob O'Bill shouted, "everyone off the site. You know who is on the tag lines. The ironworkers are already in the statue. Wait until the piece is over the top before you go out on the site."

Bob could see the pilot heading for the mountain, and he wanted to enforce Comstock's instructions about the men being off the site. When the piece was directly overhead of the last piece, we ran out and grabbed the tag lines. The wind was gusting so fiercely, we were unable to control the section. It came in backwards. The more we tried to turn it, the more the wind would push it the opposite way. Comstock could see we were having trouble, and that we were unable to maneuver the structure so the ironworkers could get a hold of it. So he lifted the section and flew away.

Steve Petersen, one of Comstock's crew, was on the site acting as radio contact. After talking with Comstock, Petersen informed us that because the winds were so strong, and the aircraft was getting low on fuel, Comstock was going to place the section on the ground in front of the statue. We had discussed the possibility of this happening in Roberts' office during briefing. It had been decided that the point in front of the statue allowed for the most room in case the situation came up. Now they were going to use this alternative. The Sikorsky came into view again, this time in front of the statue site. The piece was lowered slowly and we grabbed the tag lines, directing the piece successfully to the area designated. The hook was released, and the helicopter once again dived down the mountain heading for the airport.

The boom crane was on the mountain, but we had hoped we wouldn't have to use it as it was not large enough for the job. The crane was only used to unload our supplies and iron. Since it was all we had, operator Dave Barker moved the crane to the front where we hooked onto the section. We anticipated problems because the section was almost nine tons, and the wind was working against us. As Dave started to pick up the section, the back end of the crane rose from the ground. He had to place the section back onto the ground. Barker had little room to maneuver as he was close to the statue and the cliff was dangerously near. A group of men jumped on the back of the crane, and Dave attempted to lift the section once more. He managed to get the section high enough, but the skin was bending. Someone hollered at Dave about the wrinkling of the skin. Being under so much pressure and danger, Dave became angry and yelled, "I can't help it! I don't have enough boom!"

After many struggles, the piece finally went over the top and he was able to set it down. We all breathed a sigh of relief.

Meanwhile, Petersen, the radio man for Comstock, had been reporting what was going on to Comstock. Comstock informed us he wouldn't come back until we all knew what we were doing. The men on the mountain agreed that more instructions were welcome. They did not like the situation, either. Petersen proceeded to give the men the necessary instructions to prepare them for the next section.

The welders hurried to get the plates and gussets in place. We took turns welding and being relieved to eat. A lot of food had been donated, and when I walked into the Gingerbread Shack, I couldn't believe all the food we had. It was a feast fit for kings. Noticing Bill Barth over to one side, I went over to apologize for what had happened earlier that morning.

"I'm sorry for what I said this morning, Bill. You're right, of course, safety should come first. I just got carried away with wanting to see the statue completed. It wouldn't be worth it if someone got hurt or injured, though," I said.

We looked at each other, laughed, and shook hands. It felt good not to have this big, burly, gentle man angry with me. Vic and I sat down to eat and commented on how we would be too fat to work if we ate all that was expected of us. It tasted delicious. We'll always be grateful for all the generous donations of food the people sent to us.

Bob O'Bill came running over to the section we were welding. He asked if we would be ready for another section soon. I looked over at

Barth, grinned, and said, "How about you, Barth? Is your angle in for safety?"

He grinned back, and left to go check on the angles. On his return, he gave Bob the go-ahead to send the helicopter with the next section.

The skirting, first section on skirting, with the second section setting on the ground in front of statue.

The third section lowered by helicopter over the men situated in the second section.

The third section in place on the mountain

This time, the wind had abated and the section was placed upon the statue without any problems. The ironworkers bolted the section together and headed down the mountain for home. Feeling tired, I looked at Barth and expressed my thoughts on the possibility of getting done tonight. Barth was also dog-tired, as were the rest of the men. For two days now, we had been experiencing an emotional roller coaster and it had caught up with us. The only thing that sounded good was a good night's sleep. The wind was blowing hard again. We decided to leave the decision to the men: whether to stay and get the work done, or to do it in the morning. We gathered Vic Duran, Randy Wixsten, Jim Keane, and Wally Lindquist in the Gingerbread Shack. We put the situation to them. The wind was gusting strongly again, and snow had been predicted for the mountain areas. The men all voted to stay and finish the work, as they were afraid what might happen if the section weren't welded. I could see it was going to be a long night, and we had to be at the briefing early in the morning. I called down on the radio, and by chance asked if they could come up with more men who could weld. In about an hour, ten men showed up. I don't know where they found them, but we were sure tickled to see them. The six of us went dragging down the mountain, looking forward to a nice hot shower and a warm, comfortable bed. Before I hit the sack, I watched the news to see what they reported concerning the lift off. Marc Comstock was giving an interview on KXLF-TV.

"We were hovering in winds that were gusting over thirty-five miles per hour. That compounded our problem in trying to keep the load stable. The biggest difficulty was the crew on the ground. They had this seventeen thousand pound piece of metal which almost had air foil surfaces on it, and those winds were not allowing them to turn it so it would orient correctly."

I thought, "This was great! We were up there doing it! Now we could watch it on TV when we got home tonight."

After the interview ended, the weather came on. I was anxious to see what was in store for us weather-wise, but never did. My head was nodding, and the next thing I knew, Pat woke me up to go to bed. Yes, it had been a very satisfying day again. What would tomorrow bring?

CHAPTER THIRTY-FIVE

DECEMBER 19, 1985 - NEAR DISASTER

Feeling pretty good about the whole lift so far, I eagerly reported to Roberts' yard the next morning. Marc Comstock, the pilot, came over as I entered the office.

"You don't know how close you came to building the second base piece again," Comstock began.

"How come?" I asked surprised, as I had thought everything had gone fairly smooth.

"You told me this was to be the heaviest piece of the structure, but I underestimated the weight of it. As we picked it up, I failed to get the thrust from the chopper that we needed. The helicopter wasn't lifting as it should have. As we started across the highway, I told my winch man, Tom Bortner, to drop the piece, as I wasn't getting any lift. He radioed back that he was unable to as a Montana Highway truck was directly beneath him. I instructed him to drop the piece as soon as he was clear of the highway truck. But then I started to gain control of the machine and I yelled back over the radio not to drop it. Luckily, we were able to complete the lift."

"Thank God, you were!" I replied, shaking. "If you had dropped the section, that would have been the end of the whole project."

Later, I mentioned the incident to Earl Casagranda. He reported he had seen the truck parked on the highway. The police had stopped all traffic going onto Interstate 15, but because it was a highway truck, they had let it through. Evidently, he had stopped to watch the lift and didn't even know he had been in danger. He had possibly saved the whole project by being there. Earl and I went into the morning briefing to listen to what Comstock had to say.

"You men have to get your act together," Comstock said, starting the briefing. "It wasn't your fault the structure was so large. But from where I was in the chopper, it looked as though you were having a big tug-of-war on the site. Half was pulling one way, and the other half was going the other way. You have to all work together in turning the pieces. LeRoy, how much does the hand section weigh?"

"Around sixteen thousand pounds, or eight tons. It's a lot lighter," I replied.

"I bet!" said Comstock, thinking back on yesterday's lift.

Barth spoke up and said, "Yes, it is lighter. We weighed them."

"Is there anything I should know about this section?" Comstock asked me.

"Yes," I answered. " The hands are bolted and welded to this section. It stands on four, 4-foot posts, and once you lift off, and drop the posts, you have to place the section on the statue on the mountain. If you have to set it on the ground, you'll smash the hands."

The fourth section sitting on four legs to keep the hands off the ground. This is in Roberts Equipment yard just before liftoff.

"Can you take the hands off?" asked Comstock.

"Yes, I can cut the welds and unbolt it. We'll have to put them back on with the crane which will make it rather difficult," I reported, hoping the hands would not have to come off.

"Well," Comstock said, thinking out loud, "if it's lighter, we should be able to do it. Let's leave them on."

I smiled in relief, as I really wanted the hands to be intact. After more briefing, we left for the mountain.

Steve Peterson held another briefing for the men on the mountain concerning how to turn the section as it was being lowered to the statue. After a discussion, the men agreed to turn the section clockwise. Peterson demonstrated with his hands and body, just to make sure everyone understood the direction to turn. It was important that we were all of one mind when the piece was lowered.

Everyone felt today would go as easy as yesterday's last section had because the winds had stopped. There wasn't any breeze at all, which is quite rare for that area. We had prayed the winds wouldn't be as strong as yesterday, and from all indications, they had stopped completely. Next, we heard Connie Kenney reporting from the radio station that the hand section was on its way. Excitement once again grew, as we all assumed our positions in eager anticipation of a great lift.

As the chopper drew closer to the site, I reflected how beautiful the piece looked with the hands out. My thoughts floated back to the time I had built the first hand, and how proud I had been of it. Now here it is, going on the statue for everyone to see forever. Memories flooded back as I watched the section nearing the mountain. I was glad we didn't have to remove the hands down in the yard. It was an inspiring section, as if Mary had her hands out embracing the whole area as she flew to her resting place. Returning to the task at hand, I grabbed the tag line (along with Wally Lindquist and Ed Stepan) as the chopper hovered over us. The wind from the rotor blades was so strong, it was like being in a hurricane. My feet started to come off the ground! I looked at Wally. His were doing the same thing! My God! It felt as if the wind was going to pick us up and throw us over the cliff. Ed Stepan weighed more than Wally and me, so we pushed our backs against the statue and clung to Ed.

Something was wrong! The wind had never been this bad before. The hands were spinning out of control! The tag line was ripped from our hands and we saw the hands dip down into the statue! The ironworkers were in there! Then I noticed the chopper go down over the cliff and the hand section was swaying wildly back and forth completely out of control. I thought if the helicopter crashed, it would probable have enough fuel to explode and set the whole mountain on fire. We all left our posts now that the wind had left our area and ran frantically to the edge of the cliff, not knowing what to expect. The aircraft was still veering crazily down the mountain out of control. I prayed that the helicopter would be able to pull out of this situation without dropping the load. Comstock had made the statement that morning during briefing that if anything at all went wrong, they would have to abort the mission. The men's lives and the helicopter were too valuable to risk.

After a long moment, I noticed the chopper was regaining power and miraculously coming out of its downward spiral. I felt they were out of danger, but I was still uncertain if they would drop the hands or try to recover the careening spin they were in. Holding my breath and praying fervently, I finally breathed a sigh of relief as I saw the section straighten out and the aircraft head for an area south of town.

My attention was then diverted to the men in the statue. I heard Bob O'Bill on the CB radio reporting to the ground crew that a real problem had developed on the mountain. My first thoughts were of the men in the statue. Someone must have gotten hurt when the hand section dipped inside the statue, then rubbed along the edge of the skin before it dropped precariously over the cliff pulling the helicopter with it. Faces all around me were white with fright and men were scurrying around asking each other if they were all right. I bolted into the statue not knowing what to expect. Ron James was coming down the scaffolding.

"Was anyone hurt?" I yelled at him.

"No, but we had some close calls. Ken Schelin got tangled up in the tag line and was almost pulled out to his death. The rope came flying around his arm, then it wrapped around his neck. He managed to get them off. You can't believe the tag lines inside the statue. They were whipping out of control. One hit me, almost knocking me off the plank I was standing on. I leaped to the other plank because the hand came so close, but I missed and fell down on the crossbars. Mike Ross saw I was in trouble and grabbed me by my tool belt before I fell to the bottom." Ron related what happened, all the time shaking with the close call he had just had. His face was ashen and his eyes bright with anxiety.

After making sure everyone was safe, we all marveled that no one had been seriously injured or killed. We ran up to Peterson, who was talking to Comstock on the radio. Comstock wanted to know first of all if everyone was alright. After confirmation of no injuries except for a lump on the head, the next business was what to do with the hands hanging down from the chopper. Comstock was aware that if the hands were forced to be set down, they would experience great damage. My stomach became nauseous thinking about the damage to the hands, but then I realized that no one's life was worth losing over a piece of metal.

Comstock's voice once again came over the radio. He was running low on fuel and would be unable to unload the section on the mountain or at Roberts' yard. He was heading back to the airport.

"There go the hands," I thought to myself.

As we watched, we saw the small Huey helicopter hovering north of the Bert Mooney Airport.

"What's that little helicopter doing?" asked Randy Wixten.

"I don't know," said Vic. "Look! he's landing by the sandpit by the Mormon Church, and a couple of guys are getting out."

Just then, Comstock came back on the radio. He relayed that the support chopper has picked a spot for the section to be set down on.

A couple of the crew from the Huey aircraft ran out and grabbed the tag lines. Someone on the mountain remarked that the section had been dropped, but it looked to me like they had set it down carefully. We watched as the small chopper returned to the mountain and landed. The pilot reported that Comstock wanted Peterson down at the airport and he wanted me to come and assess the hands for damage. Peterson was dropped off at the airport while I was transported to the area in which the hands rested.

The pilot of the Huey helicopter, Blair, had reacted as soon as he saw what was developing on the mountain with the Sikorsky. As soon as he was positive that the hands were not to be aborted, he knew Comstock was going to need a place to set the section down. When He saw the mound in the sandpit, close to the airport, he knew that was the perfect spot to place the section without damaging the hands. He notified Comstock of his find, and Comstock agreed to use the area for the section.

As we neared the hands, I could see they couldn't have dropped the statue as someone reported on the mountain. One hand was resting on the ground, with minimal damage to it. I commented to Blair that Comstock had to have been extremely careful to have set the section down as well as he had. Blair agreed. As I descended from the helicopter, Earl Casagranda, John Shea, and Jim Keto greeted me. They arrived from Roberts' yard right after the crew lowered the hand section onto the mound. They were busy helping the police keep the people who resembled ants swarming over the area, away from the structure.

I climbed up the hill to determine how much destruction was done. The left hand was holding up the side of the statue. Amazed, I surveyed the damage to find the fingers weren't smashed at all --- just a few cracked welds. The right side was worse. It hung off the side of the hill and had sustained more injuries. This was the hand that had dipped into the statue when the chopper lost power. I could see how the finger followed along the skin of the statue because the whole length of the finger was smashed. Two of the fingers were crossed.

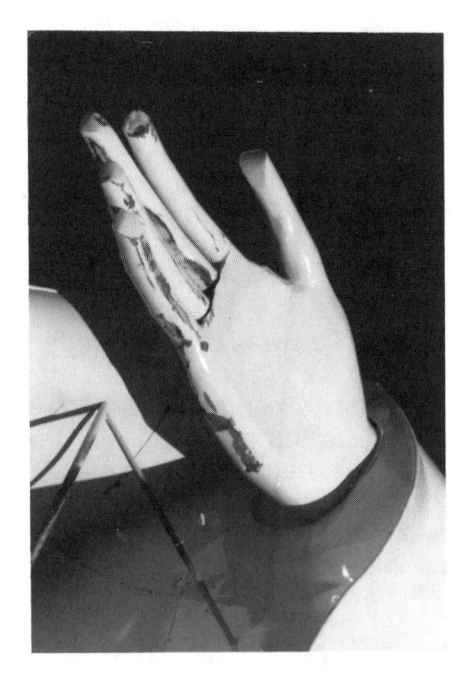

The damaged right hand after the fingers were straightened

I made the comment to Earl, "Look, she crossed her fingers so the pilots wouldn't drop her!"

"It worked!" Earl shot back.

I carefully examined the inside of the structure. Some welds were broken and some of the angle was hanging down. Nothing that couldn't be fixed, though. I figured I would have to take the hands off now, and was going to return to Roberts' yard to get the welding truck. Deciding to talk to the pilots first, I returned to the helicopter and was flown back to the airport. I conferred with Comstock and Britton. Comstock apologized for what happened.

"I almost lost part of the statue, LeRoy," he said.

"You almost lost yourselves," I stated.

"Tell me about it!" Comstock replied. "Both Britton and I were shaking when we got on the ground. Not so much for us, but for the men on that mountain."

"You guys think you were shaking!" the winchman, Tom Bortren, said still shaken up from having a ringside seat to the near disaster. "I was the one looking down on all those men and watching the hand fall in there knowing there wasn't anything I could do. As we dove off the mountain, I watched the piece almost hit the tail section of the chopper, then swing forward and almost hit the front section. It was swaying so badly, it was pushing the helicopter toward the rocks adjacent to the statue. The rotor blade just missed the cliff as we dove off. All I can say is, thank God for all the experience that Comstock and Britton received in Vietnam. Without it, we'd all be dead."

"It's a good thing we decided on our first trip up that if the aircraft had trouble, we would veer off to the left and down," Comstock stated.

"It worked," said Bortren. "My life flashed in front of me when we passed by the cliff." He couldn't believe he had come out of that one.

"Do you believe in miracles, LeRoy?" Comstock asked. I shook my head yes, thinking back on the many miracles that had already happened. "When we came up here, we weren't believers, and this was just another job to us. But now we know better. LeRoy, when we went off that mountain, we had three ways to release the hook. Manually, electrically, or we could blow the hook. All through our training, we were taught that our lives were worth more than whatever was under this chopper, and the chopper is worth millions. I could have pushed the button, the co-pilot could have pushed it, or even the winch man could have pushed it. I thought of all the work that you and all the men had done, and I couldn't push the button. I asked Britton and Bortner why they didn't push the button. They both said the same thing. They reached for the button, but couldn't push it. Wait until the National Guard Headquarters in Reno see the film that the support chopper has taken. We'll all be in trouble."

"Is that what the support chopper is here for? To take pictures?" I asked.

"That's one of the reasons," Comstock said. "We can use it for any purpose, but the films are used because it is a training exercise for others. Wait until they see this one!"

"Well, LeRoy," Comstock continued, "what do you think about the statue's hands?"

"The hands are damaged, but not beyond repair," I stated. "I can take them off, and we can repair them later. As for the rest, I'll go get the welding truck, cut the loose angle iron, and weld the cracked ones."

"Can you leave the hands on and repair them on the mountain?" Comstock wanted to know.

"No problem," I said.

"I'd like to put the statue all together on the mountain," Comstock replied. "So would the rest of the crew."

On my return with the welding truck to repair the damage, I had a problem getting to where the statue's section was. People had streamed into the area and traffic was congested. Everyone wanted to see what had happened to the hands. After much maneuvering, I managed to reach the section. Jim Keto asked me what had happened. Why did the helicopter have so much problems?

"We all prayed for no wind and were delighted that we had our prayers answered." I stated. "The pilots later informed me the wind was important to help give them the lift needed to place the section onto the statue. The cliff in front of the statue was perfect because of the updraft. Without the wind, the two gas turbine engines put out 4,500 horsepower and can lift seven tons at sea level. At this level, eight tons was the top of its capabilities according to the book. Because of the updraft of the cliff, he had been able to lift nine tons the other day. Comstock told me he won't make any more lifts until we get more wind on the mountain."

When we finished with the repairs to the hand section, I asked Tom Holter to return the welding truck to Roberts' yard while I went back to the airport to see how things were going. Comstock had been in touch with the crew on the mountain, and the winds were starting to pick up --- but not enough for another lift. I remarked that the winds usually pick up in the afternoon.

With everything done on the hand section, I was eager to return to the mountain and survey the damage that had been done when the hand dipped into the last section. Comstock sent Peterson, the radio man, with me to the small helicopter for the return trip to the mountain in case they were able to make a lift later on in the afternoon.

The men swarmed around us as we left the aircraft. They hadn't known what was going on because Peterson was at the airport, and all the news had come over the radio and the CB. We filled them in on the latest news, and reported that another lift would be possible if the winds became stronger. My first concern now was how badly the skin had been damaged on the last section. Beavis reported that Randy Wixten, Vic Duran, and Jim Keane were working on the repairs at that moment. I hurried over to the ladder, climbing it as quickly as I could. Vic saw me coming and knowing my concern, pointed to the right side of the statue's arm. It had hit the ring and bulged the side out. Randy, and Jim had already had the broken welds redone. I assessed the bulge and told them if we cut the ring and welded on a lug, maybe the come-a-long would work to pull it back to where it originally was. Trying that, we were able to secure it back almost as close as it was originally. When we placed the hand section on, we could line it up better.

Returning to the site where the men had gathered, I noticed how much the winds had picked up. Peterson was already on the radio talking to Comstock. He looked up to ascertain how hard the wind was blowing. It was judged to be around twenty-five knots at this time. Peterson then looked at the men eagerly gathered around.

"Comstock wants to know if you want him to try again," Peterson asked.

"Let's do it!" shouted two or three of the men.

"Bring it up!" yelled Vic. "We want that piece!"

Peterson grinned, relayed the message to Comstock on the radio, then turned to me.

"Comstock wants to know how bad the damage was to the section on the mountain. Can they set the hand section down on it?" asked Peterson.

"Tell him it's repaired and we're ready!" I answered.

We watched them leave the airport, then hover over the hand section still resting on the dirt mound. We lost sight of the helicopter and the section as the wind from the rotor blade caused a blizzard, picking up the snow surrounding the area. Finally the aircraft, with its load dangling beneath it, became visible again and headed for the mountain.

As it drew nearer, I became extremely nervous. I said a quick prayer to Mary for everything to go smoothly, but my nerves were still on edge. I glanced over at Vic Duran and noticed beads of sweat on his brow, even though the temperature was quite cool. My thoughts were for the ironworkers inside the structure. They were in the most danger from the rotor blades and the structure itself. Mike Cerise announced to all of us that the winds were now cresting at thirty knots, which would enable the pilots to make a good drop. Mike Cerise, Dave Barker, and Randy Wixten were on one tag line, while Wally Lindquist, Ed Stepan, and myself were on another. Seeing how nervous everyone was, I decided to crack a joke about Stepan's size.

"I bet you guys on the other side wish you had Stepan to help hold you down," I said. It worked. The other workers relaxed a little and grinned back.

In the meantime, the helicopter was coming in higher. The section started spinning again and was coming in backwards. We grabbed the tag lines hard and started to turn clockwise, just as we agreed to do the first time. The section turned quite easy, and we were able to stabilize the piece quickly. As the piece started down, we could see the snow packed on the bottom plate and knew the ironworkers would have to scrape the plates before it could be set down. When this had been accomplished, we saw the grab hooks come out and snag the tag lines. We knew the ironworkers had the section under full control. Gene Vukovich, Hoot Gibson, Ken Schelin, Lee Boggs, Tom O'Connor, Tom Vega, Bill Corcoran, Ray Nelson, Tom Carlyon, and Bill McGee could now breathe a sigh of relief. The men on the lines could now walk away and watch. I was still worried about the bulge that we pulled in and whether it was going to fit all right.

"Don't worry, LeRoy," Jim Keane reassured me. "It's going to fit this time. As the pilots set it down the bulge wouldn't let the holes line up. The pilots saw what trouble the ironworkers were having and moved the structure to help them. They were then able to bring it over. When the holes were in perfect alignment, they dropped in their spud bars. James gave Steve Peterson, the radio man, the hand signal to let it down. We could see all the holes on the robe align perfectly, so we knew the ironworkers were putting in their bolts."

All the men started celebrating.

"We did it!" Shouts went up all over the area. Joy had replaced worry on all the faces on the mountain. Men were slapping each other on the backs and running excitedly from one to the other. I realized how grateful I was to the Lord, and said a simple, "Thank you, God!"

We completed the lift just in tim, for it was getting dark soon. The ironworkers had their time in; now it was time for the welders. Mike Cerise and Al Beavis offered to stay and help, but we told them to rest up for the next day, which would make Our Lady complete.

Ron James and his crew came down and we thanked them for a job well done.

"We were all nervous," James said. "This morning was just too close and we didn't want it to happen again. We did two things to make sure of our safety. We had an escape plan just in case, and Gene Vukovich led us in prayer for our safety, the chopper, and the mission."

"It was a miracle that you men didn't get killed or hurt," I replied. "I think people in town are beginning to realize just how dangerous this mission has become."

"One thing about an ironworker," remarked Hoot Gibson, "danger is our work. Our motto is, 'No job is too tough for us.'" They now were glad to go home and relax after a very tough job, knowing they lived up to their motto.

As Jim Keane, Randy Wixten, Vic Duran, and I were welding the plates, Bob O'Bill and his electricians were hooking up lights to illuminate the work area. As soon as we got the ring in place, and the bolts in the plates welded, we headed for the Gingerbread Shack where we gulped some hot coffee, ate some John's Pork Chop Sandwiches, and Nancy's Pasties.

On the way home, Jim Keane and I were discussing what had transpired that day.

"The second try went smoothly because of the prayer," Jim commented.

"What prayer?" I asked.

"That's right, you weren't there, were you?" Jim said. "You were down with the pilots. Bob O'Bill asked me if I would lead the men in a prayer. Everyone felt it was something we needed to do before the next piece came up. Bob got his megaphone and called all the men together behind the statue. We put our arms around each other, and I said,

'We all came up here for our own reasons, and we're all dedicating ourselves to this project for whatever each of us has to offer. We're offering our skills and our abilities that we learned over the years. We thank everyone here, and we thank the One up above who brought us here. Let's bring this baby home to a happy conclusion. We need help to do that. We've got the skill, but She has to help us.'"

"It must have worked, we put it up," I replied. As we drove down the mountain, nothing much was said. We were both exhausted from the whole experience of the day.

My wife Pat was happy to see me. She had been listening to the TV reports of what had been happening, and she knew I was all right. But now she could see for herself.

On TV, Comstock had reported to Wendy Guerin, a news reporter, that all week they'd been working in pretty strong winds, but they experienced a lull in the wind that day. The piece of metal weighed about two thousand pounds less than the one they had lifted the day before. The plane had gotten to the limits and they lost power without the wind to give them the desired lift. They were almost forced to abort the mission

Pat had been watching the lift with the other teachers at work when the helicopter lost control. She had become so upset, she had to sit down and put her head on the table. She was just sure someone had been hurt during that episode. She gave a prayer of thanks when word came out that no one had been injured or killed. Since she had been home, the phone had rung constantly. People from prayer groups and all over Butte were praying for the success of the mission and for the safety of the men. All of a sudden, it became clear to me why the accident had happened. At first I had been mystified as to why Jesus and Mary hadn't been behind our efforts to put the statue up there. So many miracles and good things had happened that it was inconceivable that they wouldn't be behind the installation of the statue. As we had driven down the mountain, Jim Keane had told me about the men praying on the mountain, and now Pat was telling me the town had been on its knees to pray. Mary was trying to tell us we needed prayer, a lot of it. We prayed for wind, we got wind. We prayed for no wind, and we received none. But that was just a few of us. Now we had the whole town praying and I knew then that everything would be all right. We had PRAYER! As long as we keep prayer in what we are doing, everything would go fine.

CHAPTER THIRTY-SIX

DECEMBER 20, 1985 - TONIGHT'S PAYDAY!

As I drove to Roberts' yard, many thoughts were dashing through my mind. It was December 20, 1985. Was this the date the Lady would be completed? Would the dream come true today? How would the statue look all together? Mary built the statue, not me. It can't help looking beautiful. It's a symbol of Jesus' Mother.

I entered the office and the first person I encountered was a harried Lynn Keeley.

"Exciting, huh?" I smiled at her.

"More like a madhouse," Lynn answered me. "The phone hasn't stopped ringing. People want to know if they can help. Is everything going all right with the lifts? Can they bring some food? I've never seen the community wanting to be so involved with anything!"

"Food!" I exclaimed. "It's coming out of our ears. We won't be able to work up there. We'll be too fat!" I laughed at the idea, but thrilled with the outpouring of love and care the people were showing to the workers.

"LeRoy, you can't believe the people bringing in donations. It's overwhelming! We have stacks of checks and currency!" Lynn said. She was impressed with the amount of charity the people possessed in the city of Butte.

"Good!" I answered. "We'll need it to get the Lady finished when she is up there. Then the work really begins. This is only a very small part of the whole project."

Connie Kenney had requested an interview on the radio. I once again told the story of Bob, the promise he made, the problems we had encountered in building the structure. I was delighted to tell the listening audience how proud I was of the men and the people of Butte in supporting the whole project. Bob had also been interviewed on television. He explained the whole incident of what had happened the day before, and why it had happened. Neither of us had been prepared for all the publicity we had been exposed to.

That morning, as we drove up the interstate highway, cars were already parked off the side to watch. Word had really gotten around to all the surrounding areas, and people had come from Anaconda, Dillon, Deer Lodge, and Helena to watch the final drama about to enfold on the East Ridge. Vic Duran was relating how the city of Butte had reacted since yesterday. His sister had reported how every building in town was hooked up to the radio station. When Connie Kenney announced a lift off was in progress, everyone ran into the streets to witness the helicopter make its flight to the mountain. At the Butte Plaza Shopping Mall, you could have helped yourself to anything in the stores as the salesclerks had relinquished their duties to watch the Lady being transported to the mountain. Even the banks cleared out when the lift was reported to be in progress. School children all over the city felt a part of the excitement. Because it was so close to Christmas, whenever a lift off was announced, the students were allowed out of the classroom to view history in the making.

When we reached the top of the mountain, Bob O'Bill was already there talking to Al Beavis and Mike Cerise. We scrutinized the horizon and marveled how blue the sky appeared. We perceived it as a good omen to have such a beautiful day to finalize the completion of the Lady.

"Are you ready, LeRoy?" Beavis asked me, the excitement of the day already on his face.

"I've been ready for this day since we started!" I exclaimed. "It's hard to believe that it actually is here!"

We all gathered around the radio listening for the news that the helicopter was ready for the fifth piece to be moved. At last, we heard what we were waiting for.

"This is the fifth piece. The start of the bottom of the shoulders of Our Lady of the Rockies. Great excitement today because it's going to be beautiful picture taking. After yesterday's near mishap, we know that things are going perfectly today. Heads up everybody! Here they come! Time to run out of the courthouse, out of the Hennessy Building, and out of all those buildings uptown! Montana Power, stay alert because here they go!"

We watched the helicopter as it glided toward us following the railroad tracks. As we stood on the cliff, looking down from 8,500 feet, we noticed more cars trying to locate a place to park. All of a sudden, the aircraft turned and headed for Bert Mooney Airport. We couldn't believe it! What could have gone wrong? We ran over to Peterson, the radio man. He was talking to Comstock.

Bob O'Bill couldn't contain himself. He kept interrupting and asking, "What's wrong?" Peterson was having a hard time conversing with Comstock with all of us surrounding him.

Petersen finally accessed the story, and explained to the gathering, "Tom Bortner, the winch man, alerted Comstock of a hydraulic leak in the chopper. It was spraying fluid from the hoist system. It isn't that big of a problem, and won't take long to fix. He didn't feel comfortable taking the bust section over the men waiting in the structure because of the fluid squirting out."

We watched the Sikorsky approach the airport, wondering where Comstock would set this piece down. There would be no problem, as with the hands section, because it would set on the pads of the four legs. We observed Comstock set the section on one of the runways of the airport. The airport had the runway plowed, so there would not be the problem of swirling snow that was encountered the day before. Knowing that the lift would be delayed for about an hour, we hurried to the Gingerbread Shack to join Vic in a cup of coffee.

For the second time that morning, the bust section was airborne. We all returned to our positions, watched the helicopter climb the 8,500 feet to the top of the ridge, and hover over the last section in place. We hurried out and grabbed the tag lines. Once again, as if looking over the country before she settled in, the section was facing towards the east instead of towards the west. We rotated it easily, and Bortner lowered the bust section gently down onto the rest of the structure.

"See what prayer can do?" Vic said, referring to the prayers we had all said before the lift off took place that day.

Comstock released the hook and we were ready for the last piece. Bob O'Bill was like a cat on a hot tin roof. The excitement had built up in him like a rocket, and he was ready for takeoff himself.

"One more! One more!" he shouted excitedly, running around from one guy to another, then hurrying to the front of the statue for another quick look. Behind Bob were some of the television crew. Wanting to capture some of the excitement of the moment, Susan Peters asked Bob how he felt. She had a hard time getting his answer, as Bob had a hard time standing still.

"That was the most beautiful piece of work I've ever seen in my life. These guys are already working. We're getting ready for the other section. We want that real bad today. Believe me, it's beautiful! It's a dream come true!" Bob shouted at her as he bounced from one spot to another. Susan Peters laughed and thanked Bob, but Bob had already left for another look at the front of the statue.

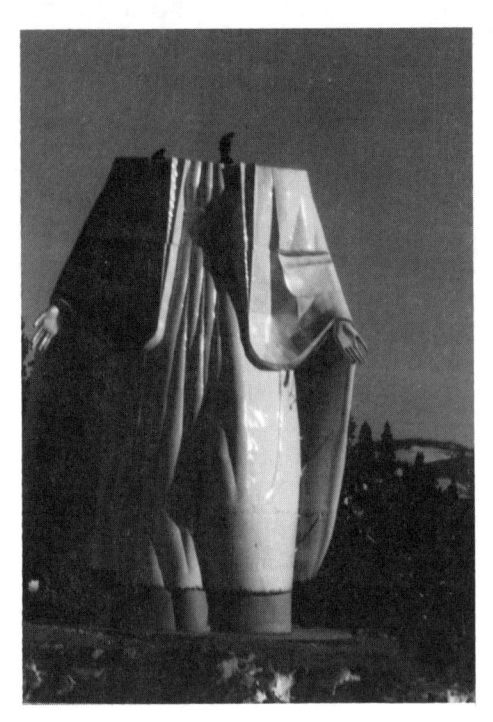

Fifth section right after installation

       The ironworkers were working industriously, and as soon as they were finished, the welders commenced attaching the plates and gussets so we could get the head section in today. While this was being done, Bill Barth was getting the wood planks up to the next section so the ironworkers would have a place to stand. When we finished the welding, we asked Ron James what the surprise was the ironworkers had hinted about the evening before. Ron just grinned and said it was something the ironworkers do on the last piece they worked on. They call it "Topping Off."
       Beavis inquired as to whether Joe Roberts would be present when the head section was installed. I didn't think anything would keep Roberts from being here. All during the last three days, Joe had been

kept busy being the "go-for." Every time Bob O'Bill would call down to George James on the CB radio, Joe would go for this, that, or whatever. Al laughed when I told him that. Here Joe was, the owner of Roberts Rocky Mountain Equipment, being used like a shop boy. Al remarked that Joe was probably in his glory with all the people down there. But he also felt that nothing would keep Joe from being on the top when the head section was installed.

Time was passing, and at this time of the year, the days were exceedingly short. We began to wonder what was keeping the last lift off. If it wasn't to be soon, they wouldn't be able to make it before it got dark. Just as we were beginning to doubt whether the second lift of the day would take place, the radio announced that the head section was about to be airborne. Bob O'Bill gathered all the men behind the statue.

"LeRoy," Bob asked. "Will you say something?" I took the bullhorn and witnessed each man taking another by the hand. I thought back to the conversation Jim Keane and I had going down the mountain. Then I knew what I wanted to say.

"When they set the hands down on the mound below, my heart fell. I went down to look at how much damage was done. When I came back on the mountain, I was sick. I asked Mary why she did this. I couldn't understand. She had done so much for the project. Then as I was going home, Jim Keane told me you took each others hands, and prayed. I knew then that she had you all pray together. This was the first time this group had ever prayed together and I knew then why the accident had happened."

Bob then handed the bullhorn to Jim Keane. "Will you please say something, Jim?" Bob asked.

Jim took the horn, lowered his head, then started in slowly: "Looking back two weeks ago, it was twenty below zero, and no one thought this project had a chance, including me. But here we are. We've got everything we've asked for all week long. We've got weather we can work with and it's just been beautiful. Those ironworkers don't like to work in the wind, so they prayed for no wind yesterday, and we got that. They decided we needed wind. We prayed for that and we got wind in the afternoon. We got up this morning, we prayed for wind, and it's been perfect all day! So Mary, we just put the section with your heart in it the last time, and now we are going to put your head on to complete this project. So, let's do it!!" Everyone gave a loud, resounding cheer, and confidence was at an all-time high.

Al Beavis asked me, "How much does the head section weigh?"

"Not that bad; about six tons. It's the lightest piece of the statue. The chopper shouldn't have any trouble at all," I said.

I turned around and noticed Jack Warner from the shop over to the side. I felt bad, because he was here and the other guys from the shop weren't able to be. It wouldn't have been so bad, but Jack never did believe in the statue or that it would ever be here. The other guys had all believed and had taken part in some part of the construction of her. Maybe another miracle was about to take place, and Jack would become a believer!

Susan Peters had interviewed Joe Roberts after the bust section had been successfully installed. Joe had been moved to tears. He was a very sentimental person, and he expressed his feelings about the whole experience.

"It was fantastic, as usual. Everything went smooth, and seems to be going just right. It's a day that's hard to believe, as far as I'm concerned. Bob and I know we'll never see another one. It's just a little tough today, you know. This is five years! The greatest bunch of guys I've ever met in my life." Joe's eyes teared, and he had a hard time keeping the lump out of his throat.

As I looked around, I noticed Joe Roberts, Bob O'Bill, and others had their wives and relatives up here. They had told us at the morning briefing at Roberts that no one would be allowed on the mountain but the men who would be working because of the danger. I would have loved to have had my wife Pat here. She had been involved from the start of the statue, always encouraging me, and making me believe in myself.

Thinking of Earl Casagranda, I walked over to Joe Roberts. "Did Earl talk to you about coming up in his Santa Claus suit?" I asked him.

"Yes, I thought it would be a good idea since it is so close to Christmas," Joe answered.

I had seen Earl last evening on his way to a party for children. Every year he dresses up and plays Santa for whomever asks him. I thought at the time that when the helicopter comes in to the site, he should walk out and wave to the pilots. They didn't want anyone on the site, but who can say no to Santa? Earl liked the idea, but he said he wouldn't do it unless he had Roberts' approval.

"Here comes Earl, now," Joe said, pointing to the pickup that had just arrived. "See if he brought his suit."

Earl had indeed brought his suit, and was going into the statue to change so he would be ready when the pilots neared the site

As the head was lifted from the yard, the Boulevard Fire Department sounded their siren in salute to the last section. Other people took their cue from them, sounded their horns, and yelled as the head swayed gently over them. Church bells rang as people rejoiced in the streets, celebrating the final lift off. George James, manning the CB radio at Roberts, reported the jubilant people were hugging and clapping each other on the backs. Everyone felt so much a part of the project. And they were! They all donated time, money, and food. Furthermore, their emotions were caught up with the joys, problems, and worries connected to the five-year project. It was a complete community project.

Sikorsky Skycrane transporting the head section over the city of Butte, Montana

Watching the chopper coming up the ridge with the head of Our Lady was a memorable sight. She swung around as if to survey the whole area which she was about to reign over. I swore there was a smile on her face as she gently advanced toward the mountain site. A lump in my throat became larger as she came nearer. On top of her head was the ironworkers surprise --- a Christmas tree and the American flag. As the head came in, it turned to the left, then to the right. Then she turned and looked at all the men standing behind the Gingerbread Shack taking pictures. There were television crews from KXLF and KTVM of Butte, KSL and KUTV of Salt Lake, and NBC News. It was as if the Lady posed for them all.

Then she slowly turned and looked at Butte, her reign about to begin. Just then, Earl Casagranda came out of the statue in his Santa Claus suit and waved at the pilots. Comstock radioed down to Peterson.

"Is that Santa Claus down there on the site, or did we have too much to drink last night?" he said.

Peterson radioed back, "No, you're not seeing things. It's the Old Boy, himself." Everyone, even the pilots, got a laugh out of it. It was a very special touch, and one that touched us all.

Santa Claus (Earl Casagranda) waving to the helicopter crew.

There wasn't anything the tag line crew could do for this section. All the lines were inside of the shoulders. It was completely up to the ironworkers. It was like someone putting a cup over you. That was how the ironworkers felt as the head descended on them. Steve Peterson, the radio man, was on top of the rocks to the right of the statue. James stood at the bottom and gave hand signals to him. The ironworkers inside would relay to the other workers half way down, and he'd relay down to one at the bottom to James. James would then signal to Tom Bortner, and he would lower the head. As it came down, the ironworkers had to lay on their backs due to the lack of space. When it was down, James had to inform Peterson to lift it up again because it was hitting one of the ladders. Bortner lifted it, and they took the cutting outfit and cut it out. Once that was completed, James informed Peterson and Bortner to set it down in place.

Connie Kenney, from KBOW radio, announced to the waiting public as soon as she saw the Skycrane release the hook, "It looks like they have it into position once again. Oh, the cable has been dropped, and that means the statue is in place. Our Lady of the Rockies is now complete!"

There was no way I was going up inside of the statue and start welding. I had to see what Our Lady looked like complete. The back looked great and I was pleased. Everything fit. From the first day, I worried that something wouldn't fit. I thought of each piece, one on top of the other, and they had never been all together before. I ran out in front of her. Jim Keane was hugging someone. I grabbed them both and gave them a big hug. Together, we looked up into the most beautiful sight we'd ever seen.

Our Lady of the Rockies! She was now complete! We looked at each other and raised our hands just as if we had won an immense victory. All the men were giving me a hug and telling me how beautiful she was. And she was --- breathtakingly beautiful! All the ironworkers came running down from inside the statue to the front. As I looked at them, they all had tears in their eyes. I told them thanks for helping put up this extraordinary lady. They all thanked me for letting them be part of this wonderful miracle. Al Beavis came over and hugged me. I wanted to ask him if it was worth all the long days and nights that were put into road. But before I could say anything, Mike Cerise came over and hugged us both. Then Mike gathered a group of men together. They put their arms around each other and said a prayer of thanksgiving.

As the Sikorsky flew over before going to the airport, we all gave them a thumbs up signal. I felt sad for them. Here we were hugging and congratulating each other, while they were heading back to the airport instead of being able to rejoice with us. I knew they were doing their own celebrating inside of the aircraft.

Our Lady is complete and starting her reign sitting on top of the Continental Divide.

A back view of the completed statue overlooking the city of Butte, Montana with her arms open.

    I stepped back to where Bob O'Bill and Joe Roberts were standing. I threw my arms around them embracing them together. All this time, I had been saying things I had no recollection of. But when I encompassed these two men, I said, "Oh, boy, guys! We did it! We did it! Oh, it's beautiful!! Did you go out and look at it, Joe?"
    Joe had been overcome with emotion, and could only shake his head no. "Oh, Come on, go!" I blurted out, pushing him towards the

front of the statue. As Joe looked up, his face beamed with happiness, and an enormous smile covered his countenance.

"Oh, sweet Jesus," he murmured, unable to take his eyes from her.

"Isn't that something? I'm so proud!" I whispered softly, feeling as emotional as Joe did. Just then, one of the television announcers grabbed me, breaking into my reverie. He asked me how I felt. How do you describe that kind of feeling? I answered the best I knew how.

"Am I excited?" I said. "Oh, if the people of Butte aren't proud now, they should be. Oh, I'm so proud of these people of Butte. I just can't express it! I am so thrilled! Everyone of those people down there should be proud. They are all a part of it. For every piece of iron I put in it, there was one person standing behind me. I am so thrilled!" I kept repeating the same thing, as I really couldn't express what the feeling was inside of me except pride in everyone believing in the project.

Then the reporter noticed Roberts standing in front of the statue, teary-eyed with emotion. He asked Joe the same question. "How do you feel?"

"Oh, I can't believe it, you know! Well, it's hard to take. All these years! The years weren't so bad, but when you see all these guys, you know, and gals too. For five years they've done everything! The people of Butte are the greatest in the world. Got hearts like you can't believe, and love very deeply! It was a beautiful dream come true! It was worth all the years! To think it at last has come true!" Joe was so overcome with emotion, he could no longer say anything. All he could do was stare at the white edifice in front of him.

One of the men standing by Bob remarked that the statue looked like a million, and all Bob could do is look up and say how beautiful she was. Joyce, his wife, was standing at his side, and all she could say was, "Yes! Yes!"

"It was worth it!" said Bob, "It was worth it!"

I walked over to Joyce, and giving her a big hug, whispered to her, "Because of you, Joyce, all because of you!"

"No," whispered Joyce in my ear.

"Yes! Yes!" I insisted. "You were the chosen one!" As I hugged Joyce, I thought of what a wonderful miracle Mary had performed here on the mountain. Because of Joyce and Bob's promise to Mary, all the wonderful things Mary has done has indeed been a dream come true. This whole undertaking had been one of God's miracles to show us what faith, love, and determination can accomplish. So many things had happened during these five years: from the beginning of Bob's promise, to all the trials and tribulations during the construction of the statue, to now, the glorious completion of His Mother's likeness.

As I looked over at Joe Roberts with tears in his eyes and a smile on his face, I thought back to the time when he told me to never use the word "miracles." I wondered if Joe would call this a miracle?

When Earl and the others had come up on the mountain, they brought some champagne donated by Bob and Joe Wholesale. One of the men broke a bottle open on the iron of the Lady and everyone gave a cheer. As everyone was celebrating, Mike Cerise told about his little boy.

"My son asked me one night after I came down off the mountain, when I would get paid. I told him the night the lights are turned on the statue," Mike related.

Bob, with his arm around Mike, tears welling in his eyes, shouted, "Tonight's payday! Today's payday!"

As we were standing around enjoying the moment, we heard the Huey helicopter coming up the mountain. We knew it was Comstock, Britton, and Bortner. When they landed, we all ran to shake their hands and to congratulate them for a job well done. We handed them a bottle of champagne, and they took a victory drink with us after they went out to the front of the statue. Comstock shook my hand and patted me on the back.

"It's an honor to know you," Comstock said sincerely, pumping my hand.

"I will never forget you, either," I solemnly stated. The sun was starting to go down and everyone hated to see the day end. I became anxious to get home to share with my family since they were not on the mountain with everyone else. Roberts told us all to be at the Safeway parking lot at six o'clock. The city was presenting us with a fire truck ride through town.

"What's that?" Comstock asked, puzzled.

"The city does that for all the athletes when they win a championship. It's a victory ride and they've been doing it for years. It's quite an honor. They must feel we are in the champion class for what we have done," I explained to him.

We headed on down the mountain, and the men with me were brought to Roberts' yard where their vehicles were. I started to drive home across the highway, and as I looked up at the mountain, I was overcome with emotion once more. There stood Our Lady of the

Rockies all lit up, keeping watch over our city of Butte. Bob O'Bill and the electricians had remained on the mountain to make sure the Lady was lit up for all to see. Many times I had driven down the highway and looked at the black mountain against the skyline. Now, to see Our Lady as a guiding light for travelers standing there with the light shining on her, I once more became choked up. It looked as if she was standing in the sky. My eyes filled with tears. I could only whisper, "Thank you, God! Praise you, Lord!" I couldn't stop crying. I could barely make out the road in front of me. Somehow, I managed to get to my back door, where I collapsed in an emotional heap.

"What's the matter?" my wife Pat kept asking me. She had never seen me in this state before, and all sorts of terrible things had run through her mind. She was sure someone had gotten killed or hurt on the mountain. I couldn't even answer her, I was crying so hard. Frightened, she managed to get me into the bedroom, thinking she would have to call a doctor. Finally, I was able to convey to her that everything was all right physically, and that no one had gotten hurt. After a few moments, I managed to get some control of myself to ask, "Why me, Pat? Why me? Why was I chosen to build this statue of God's Mother? I'm a nobody."

Pat gently put her arms around me, saying, "God always picks on nobodies. Mary was a nobody until God picked her. The children at Fatima were nobodies until Mary called them. The same thing at Lourdes. Why not you?"

I felt much better after talking with Pat. We drove down to Safeway's lot on Harrison Avenue, where the fire truck was waiting for all the workers. Many times I had watched as the fire engine gave high school champions a ride down Harrison Avenue. Never did I imagine I would be doing this at my age. As we drove down Harrison and then uptown, the people came out waving at us. The helicopter crew laughed and said they had never dreamed they would ever do something like this. We were glad to disembark, as the temperature had dropped to below zero, and the wind was really cold. This was something we would never forget. The whole day was like a dream come true. Like Bob and Mike said: "Today's payday!"

The day wasn't over yet, though. When we returned from the fire truck ride, we were informed there was going to be a reception for everyone at the Copper King Inn. People streamed into the pool side convention room to meet the workers and the pilots. I gave each of the helicopter crew a cross which I had been making from the scrap metal of the statue. Comstock came over to talk.

"Remember you were going to tell me something, but wanted to wait until the statue was completed?" I mentioned to him.

"Are you sure you want to know?" he said teasing me.

"Can't hurt now," I said.

"Down in Reno, Nevada, we were hauling a six track," said Comstock, "when the cable on the winch slipped and dropped fifteen to twenty feet. It hit so hard, it damaged a gear. We had one on order and was hoping we would have it in before we took on this project. We didn't get it and hoped and prayed it wouldn't do it again."

"I'm glad you didn't tell me," I said. "I would have been worried sick when you brought up the head if I thought the cable might slip."

They were all nice guys, and I was proud to know them. I shared some things about the statue and what Mary had done. They had come here just to do a job. It was just a project to them. Now they had all become believers. They felt they had seen many miracles happen here in Butte, Montana.

"I'll never forget Butte and its people," Comstock remarked. "The statue will be in my heart forever. I only wish we didn't damage the hand."

"There's something about the hand," I said. "The Lady is trying to tell us something. The small ceramic statue I used to build the statue from had the right hand damaged. Then we had small statues made to sell, and the hands cracked and would break off. We had commemorative buckles made, and again the right hand was breaking off. A few workers had their hands hurt working on the statue, and now the Lady herself has damaged hands."

"That's weird," said Comstock.

"Yeah," I agreed. "The hand was the first thing I built using scrap iron. When the people saw the hand, the donations started to come in to build the rest of the statue. I think what the Lady was trying to tell us was not to be afraid to put out our hands and ask for what we need. So we did. This alone was a miracle because Butte was at the lowest point in its history. Everyone was out of work, yet people took their hands and reached into their pockets to give what little they had. Mary also showed us what the power of prayer can do."

"You're right," replied Comstock. "Once everyone prayed, everything went fine."

CHAPTER THIRTY-SEVEN

THUMBS UP!

Saturday morning came, and reluctantly, I climbed out of bed. Exhaustion still claimed me from the night before, but I was deeply aware of what needed to be done to prepare the Lady to withstand the harsh winter ahead. Driving over to Roberts' yard, I speculated on whether many workers would help with the Lady now that the structure was assembled. When I arrived, I was pleasantly surprised. Many willing hands greeted us, still eager to help. One of the men reported the helicopter crew were planning to return to Reno, Nevada, that afternoon to be with their families for Christmas.

We drove up the mountain and welded until noon. Then, as we gathered in the Gingerbread Shack for lunch, Earl Casagranda heard the sound of a helicopter. We all bolted out to see who it was. Just as I suspected, it was the Sikorsky Skycrane. The crew had come to say good-bye and to take one last glimpse of the beautiful edifice they had helped situate on the mountain. They flew around the back, and then circled to the front. I was standing on the large rock on the left side of the statue. The aircraft hovered in midair. They were so close, I felt I could jump in with them. The crew smiled and signaled with their thumbs up. Caught by the moment and with a feeling of gratitude in my heart, I saluted them with the utmost sincerity. The mosquito shaped aircraft lunged to the west and flew towards Roberts' yard before taking their final departure to Reno. Turning back towards the men standing behind me, I noticed they still had their thumbs up, and tears were welling in their eyes. Our hearts, prayers and thanks had gone out to the men who manned the Sikorsky Skycrane from Reno, Nevada. For four days, our lives had been intertwined in a very rewarding encounter.

LeRoy Lee saluting pilots as they depart for Nevada

Later in the day, Bob O'Bill and Joe Roberts drove up with their wives and families. After that, they brought caravan after caravan of people to view the Lady close up.

Early Sunday morning, Bob O'Bill woke me out of a sound sleep to ask if I was going on the mountain again. I replied that I was, but not until I went to church to give thanks for the past week. Bob remarked that I could give thanks on the mountain just as easily, but that wasn't my way of doing things any more. At one time of my life, it would have been, but not now, after all that has happened. In church that morning, Father Gary Reller, the pastor, remarked to the congregation how beautiful the Lady looked on the mountain, and how many workers there were in church that morning. As a testimonial to them, everyone clapped and the tape of "Our Lady of the Rockies" by Mark Staples was played. As I stood there with the other men scattered around the church, I felt prouder than ever to be part of the whole project. Looking around, the large church seemed fuller than it usually would be.

Later, I mentioned the large crowd to parishioners from other churches and faiths, and found all of them had been filled to capacity that Sunday. Butte is a faith-filled community and they know how to say thanks to the Lord. Since the Lady has been established on the mountain, many of the churches have experienced a revival of faith from their people. More and more people have endeavored to attend services on Sunday every week, and even during the week. This was another miracle from the Lady, I believe.

After Mass on Sunday, I accompanied my wife, my daughter Cindy and her husband Del, and our grandchildren, Travis and Chad, to view the structure on the mountain. They were awestruck. Her immense size was overwhelming. Del and I stayed to work on her, while the rest of the family returned to the valley.

Monday, Bob O'Bill invited me to his house at 6:30 in the evening. I wasn't told the reason, but when I arrived, Al Beavis, Mike Cerise, Bob O'Connor, and Billy Fisher were there, too. I discovered Pat Kearney from KXLF-TV was going to interview the group for his video slated for viewing on New Year's Eve. I tried to enlist Bob's help to tell some of the happenings that had occurred on the mountain, but Bob vetoed that strongly. He felt this was not the proper time to reveal them. The other fellows felt the same way, but I was disappointed. To me they are what the Lady is all about, but I concurred with the consensus. The video went well, and we were all anxious to see it in its entirety on New Years Eve.

Christmas Day arrived. The phone didn't stop ringing with people wanting to go on the mountain. Pat refused to let me out of the house, saying this was a family day, and I needed the rest. She was right, although I don't know how much benefit the family received from my presence. I fell asleep every time I sat in my big easy chair. I tried to watch the ball games, or to talk to Pat or one of the kids, but all I could do was sleep. I didn't realize what the past week had taken out of me. All day long, I either was sleeping or going to the window to see if the Lady was really there. In some ways, it all felt like a dream.

On New Years Eve, everyone was anxiously waiting to view the video Pat Kearney had made of the Lady of the Rockies. We were not disappointed. It was excellent! Tears came to my eyes many times as I recalled all the incidents related to the making of the statue.

We had always said that the day the Lady goes on the mountain will be the day Butte's economy will rebound. Already it had been revealed that Dennis Washington, a wealthy businessman from Missoula, Montana, had bought the mines from ARCO, and they were about to be reopened. Many businesses had sprung up, and Butte did seem to be experiencing a comeback in economy. Putting the statue up on the mountain showed the rest of the state of Montana that Butte still had determined people who did not lie down and die. They proved that by pulling together, they can accomplish miracles. Pat captured on his video how the people themselves can determine their destiny.

    Al Beavis, Bill Barth, and I met on the mountain a few weeks later. We knew this would be the last time we would be there until next spring. After all, we had remained on the mountain about a month longer than usual. It was still winter, and winter in Montana can be quite harsh. We spent the day installing the new gate I had built. The snow was falling rapidly, but for sentimental reasons, we weren't concerned about it. We all wanted to make this day last as long as we could. It would be a long time until we could once again work on Our Lady. Now we could only watch her light from down below. We all felt The Lady was there to watch over all of us.

To reorder Our Lady Builds a Statue, send $10.00 for book Plus shipping and handling $5.00 to

LeRoy Lee
2845 Nettie
Butte, MT 59701

For more information about Our Lady of the Rockies call
1-800-800-5239